Summoning My Inner Ballerina

Balancing Love and Loss, Family and Friends, Life and Politics

By Paula Mack Smith

iUniverse, Inc.
Bloomington

Summoning My Inner Ballerina
Balancing Love and Loss, Family and Friends, Life and Politics

iUniverse books may be ordered through booksellers or by contacting:

iUniverse
1663 Liberty Drive
Bloomington, IN 47403
www.iuniverse.com
1-800-Authors (1-800-288-4677)

ISBN: 978-1-4759-4970-4 (sc)
ISBN: 978-1-4759-4971-1 (hc)
ISBN: 978-1-4759-4972-8 (e)

Library of Congress Control Number: 2012916754

Printed in the United States of America

iUniverse rev. date: 9/14/2012

Contents

To Neil

Still crazy about you
After all these years

Preface

Like so much of life, this book came about by accident. In the fall of 2011, the *Miami Herald* conducted a "flash" writing contest. The subject was living in South Florida. I wrote my entry, "Leaving Winter Behind," in short order. Much to my dismay, I didn't win, but while writing my story, I realized how much I had missed the creative process, the act of putting my thoughts onto paper. And so, I quit my "day job" as volunteer president of my Florida condominium and began to put my life into print, through a series of personal stories. I e-mailed them to friends and family, who encouraged me and shared their own life experiences and, sometimes, secrets, with me in return.

Writing is such an interesting process, almost impossible to describe to outsiders. I can't remember a time when I didn't love to write. In my youth, it took the form of diaries and letters to various "pen pals." Later it would be term papers, which I thoroughly enjoyed writing, particularly when the topic was something I really cared about. Eventually, I became a journalist, writing about Long Island and its people, especially its people.

When I write, the ideas and words appear in my brain and I scramble to put them on paper or type them onto my computer before they slip away. Then I re-write and edit and hone the work until it is as perfect as possible, as true as can be to the reality that I am trying to express. Inspiration comes from a variety of sources. An old photograph, a headline, a dream, a rock and roll lyric, a distant memory. When it comes, I grab the nearest piece of paper and begin to write.

This book's title eluded me for the longest time. And then I remembered a photo taken when I was ten. The picture used to embarrass me. I was such a skinny little thing in my ballerina costume. The makeup, especially the dark red lipstick, looked out of place on my childish features. But the little girl in the photo was completely unaware of how she looked to anyone else. She felt like a princess. She felt total confidence. She felt like she could conquer the world.

Now I look at that little girl with awe and a fierce love. She is a part of me, maybe the best part of me. And so I named this book for her, my inner confident ballerina.

The Confident Ballerina

She stands erect, arms raised in a perfect arc, feet carefully positioned. A proud smile adorns her face, her lips painted crimson against her pale skin, her stick-straight hair permed for this special occasion. Her slender form is dressed in a costume, painstakingly made by her mother, consisting of a hot pink satin top and matching tulle skirt, gaudily adorned with black sequins. Topping it off is a matching headdress. It, too, is made of pink satin and black sequins, tied in a neat bow under her chin.

I was ten when I posed for this photo, the only picture of me from my childhood where I appeared alone, without any siblings. It was the night of my first dance recital and I felt like the most beautiful little girl in the world. I was utterly self-possessed. That feeling would pass just a few short years later, when puberty came knocking and my body shot up to its present 5'10" height, and, out of nowhere, breasts appeared. These events caused me to develop a permanent slouch and a crushing self-consciousness about my body, which would last throughout my teenage years. I would not feel comfortable in my own skin until eight years later, when I left home for college.

Numerous times in the years since that recital, I have had to call upon my inner "confident ballerina" for the strength to help get me through times of stress and loss and challenges. Challenges as daunting as the suicide of my best friend at twenty-one, handling cancer diagnoses (my own and my husband's), the fire that destroyed our Long Island home in 2009, and the near-fatal illness of our older son eight years ago. But I have also had to summon her on numerous less dire circumstances, like a dreaded root canal procedure, and fleeting panic attacks as I walked into a high school reunion, and a casual get-together with the other mothers from the neighborhood elementary school shortly after we moved to Upper Brookville in 1977. In the latter instance, I actually drove up to the restaurant but could not bring myself to walk through the front door. I got back into my car, drove home, composed myself and returned a few minutes later. "Didn't I see you at the door a few minutes ago?" inquired one of the mothers. "Yes. I forgot something at home," I replied. What I didn't tell her, what I have never admitted to anyone before now, is that what I sorely needed at that particular moment in time was to summon up my inner "confident ballerina." She has always come through for me, that spunky little ballerina with her sunny, optimistic outlook on life.

My stint as a ballerina was brief. But for that one night, I felt like a star, a diva before the term was invented. It is fortunate that no video survives of that recital, for I was an awkward child with poor balance, possibly the result of an ice skating accident at an early age. Or perhaps I was just a child with no natural dancing skills or grace. It didn't matter. What mattered most in that one shining moment in the spotlight was the confidence I felt, the knowledge that I was special and worthy of the attention and applause of the audience beyond the footlights.

I could have danced all night.

Love and Marriage

I have been married for more than two-thirds of my life. To the same man, I might add. It is hard for me to remember a time when I wasn't married and our marriage wasn't a central fact of my identity. It doesn't encompass all of who I am or define me. I've had many roles to play in my life. But our marriage is still at the center of my being.

Because of its importance in my own life, I can completely empathize with people who also wish to marry but can't because their intended is the "wrong" race or religion or gender. Love is love. Marriage is marriage. Why any two people who are head over heels in love should be denied the right to marry is beyond my comprehension. It is just a matter of time before the so-called "Defense of Marriage Act" is repealed and rightly so. It defends nothing. It is legalized discrimination, pure and simple.

I dedicate this book to my husband, Neil, for many reasons, but the most important one is that he has played the central role in my life since we first met in 1965. He is my leading man. Whether the news is good or bad, it doesn't seem real to me until I share it with him. The few times we've been apart for more than a day seemed unreal, something no amount of phone calls could make up for. Is he my everything? No. Friends and family and others are very important to me. But is he the most important person in my life? Absolutely.

"Can't Help Myself"

I didn't date much at all in high school. I remember it as a three-year period of waiting for college. Waiting for my real life to begin.

Choosing a college was easy. I fell in love with politics during the 1960 Democratic convention, so Washington, D.C. was a no-brainer. After visiting the schools there and reading the brochures, the obvious choice was American University. What a patriotic name! Such a beautiful campus! American University it was.

Freshman year was a whirl of social activity. I was out on the town almost every night. Boys from George Washington University and Georgetown came courting. Once I dated a student from A.U. only to find out later that I had become known on campus as "the tall skinny chick that dates Ira Gelnick." I was truly horrified, as I wanted to be known for myself, not for whom I was dating. So A.U. boys were then crossed off my list of potential dates.

Midway through freshman year, I went out with a G.W. student known as "Potter" to a party in a house on Dupont Circle. The date ended badly and I left the scene in a huff, planning to catch a bus back to campus. *Men! I muttered to myself.* A fellow guest offered me a ride home. His name was Neil. He called the next day and asked me out for the following weekend. The night before our date, my roommate Anna and I stayed up all night working on the congressional campaign of one of our political science professors. Dead tired the next morning, I tried to contact Neil to reschedule the date, but didn't know which dorm he lived in at G.W. So I resigned myself to making an appearance and keeping the date as short as possible.

Luckily, it turned out to be a great first date. He made me laugh. The conversation flowed easily. We kissed in the rain. I forgot how tired I was, and we barely made it home before the midnight curfew (yes, dorms had curfews in the mid-1960s). We continued to date regularly for several months, but when other boys called, I accepted dates with them, too. I was keeping my options open.

And then came Spring Weekend at G.W. A romantic cruise on the *S.S. George Washington* down the Potomac River. A visit to an amusement park, complete with bumper cars and vast quantities of cheap draft beer. On the return cruise to the pier, we searched for a quiet place to get away from the rowdy crowd, discovering an empty lifeboat on a lower deck. We nestled together in the bottom of the boat just holding one another. I remember feeling safe and warm with his arms around me. His facade of self-confidence was betrayed by a little tremor in his left leg, which I found incredibly endearing.

That was it. I never went out on a date with anyone else. I was thoroughly smitten. The die had been cast. Before long, we had a song, our song. It was "Can't Help Myself" by the Four Tops. It's been 47 years since Spring Weekend. I'm still smitten and I still can't help myself.

Whole Lotta Love

I have never understood people who enter into a marriage with doubts. If you are not sure, marriage isn't the cure. Marriage is hard. It's work. If you don't enter into it crazy in love with your spouse, in all likelihood, it won't last. Somewhere, some day, you'll meet your "soul mate," the person you can't live without, and then you'll face really difficult choices, especially if children are involved.

It is a matter of simple arithmetic. If one and one equal two, walk away, because when it comes to romantic relationships, one and one need to add up to ten, or a hundred, or, if you're really lucky, a million. If it is just two, you are settling, and you'll be sorry some day.

I knew early on that Neil and I were so much greater than the sum of our parts. My mom used to worry about us. "What will happen when one of you dies?" she'd ask me, only half-joking. "How will you manage without the other?" This from the woman who had opposed our marriage in the beginning on religious grounds. I never knew how to answer that question, because, truthfully, I have no idea. With any luck, we'll be together for many more years and then die simultaneously.

Until then, we are together as we struggle through life, always there for each other, through thick and thin, sickness and health. Spontaneously combusting on a regular basis.

The two of us, so much greater than the sum of our parts.

The two of us, poolside at Mystic Pointe

Going to the Chapel

Our wedding day dawned sunny and warm. That wouldn't be unusual except for the fact that it was January in Northern New Jersey. As a result, we had the photographer take plenty of pictures outdoors, both outside the Glen Rock Jewish Center, where the ceremony was held, and outside our family home on Harding Road, where we held the reception. The white mink stole that I borrowed from Momma Nancy for the occasion remained unworn as the temperature reached a balmy seventy degrees. I was a little disappointed because it looked great with the dress, an Alfred Angelo design I bought the previous summer using my Bamberger's employee discount.

I had a brief "bridezilla" moment when the photographer arrived at our house before the ceremony and I imperiously sent him on his way. Also, to my eternal shame, I yelled at my best friend Kathy for ignoring my explicit instructions by wearing her hair up instead of down. What nerve! In short, I was a basket case until we arrived at the temple and I caught sight of Neil. From that moment on, I just couldn't stop smiling. During the ceremony. At the reception. I was one happy bride. Ron was our best man (and still is) and his toast was memorable. "To Paula and Neil. You just know they're gonna be happy."

A lot of our college friends arrived by bus from Manhattan. As it turns out, Neil's Uncle Sol and Aunt Selma were on the same bus and they led the group in song. All in all, it was a joyous and memorable occasion. It was followed by a larger, more traditional reception at my in-laws' home in Peekskill the following weekend.

We've been to more weddings than I can count in the years since, each unique in its own way. Ron and Mai Mai's wedding included two receptions, one of which was an elaborate banquet in Chinatown. Neil is still talking about the food at that one. Then there was a strange wedding held at Leonard's of Great Neck. The mother of the bride was a relative of Neil's on his mother's side. She got a bit tipsy at the cocktail hour before the ceremony and confided to us that the bride wasn't in love with the groom. Talk about a conversation stopper!

There was an even more bizarre scene at another wedding, this time in Brooklyn. I was in the ladies' room when I overheard the groom's mother and her daughter discussing the difficulty they were having getting a bloodstain off the mother's fancy gown. I exited the stall and asked if I could be of help and how this had happened. I was told that one of the guests had gotten into a fight outside the banquet hall and was stabbed. When he came back inside, he asked the groom's mother to dance. *Hence the blood on her dress.* I left the ladies' room rather hastily and returned to the table to find Neil and relay this odd story. "Where's Neil?" I asked our tablemates. "He just stepped outside for some air," came the reply. Just before I fainted dead away, Neil reappeared, unharmed and oblivious to the goings-on.

We've been to fancy weddings at exclusive country clubs. At one of these, in Rhode Island, Neil impulsively suggested to the woman sitting next to him, the sister of the groom's mother, who is a close friend of ours, that they both let their hair down. His was in the usual loose ponytail. Hers was in a tidy bun. She turned away from him without answering. Ouch! Needless to say, no one let his or her hair down at *that* affair. We also attended an Orthodox Jewish wedding in Brooklyn where Neil and I had to sit apart. This was not fun for us but seemed acceptable to the rest of the guests. On another occasion, we attended a wedding at New York's City Hall where we were the only witnesses. It didn't feel like a wedding at all. It was all so perfunctory, even sad.

One of our all-time favorite weddings was that of my niece Julie, who married her best friend Brian in Vermont in the summer of 2010. The groom was quite a bit older than Julie and the wedding was officiated by his son, the young pastor of a local church. It was the most personal of ceremonies with the pastor movingly paying tribute both to his dad and the bride, whom he had known for many years. Like her Aunt Paula, Julie never stopped smiling through the entire affair. She was one happy bride.

Our Wedding, 1967: Anna, Marci, Neil, me, Ron, and Kathy

Our Marital Bed

Every marriage has occasions when the bond is tested. Our first test came about five months after the wedding.

Neil and I were married between semesters of his senior year (my junior year) of college and we lived off-campus in an apartment in Arlington, Virginia. It was modestly furnished with used furniture, which we gladly left behind when we moved to New York after he graduated in June of 1967. He was following in the footsteps of his two older brothers by going into the family business at Fulton Fish Market. His parents had recently moved into a new home in Peekskill, New York, near Pine Lake Park. Their town house in Jackson Heights was available for our use rent-fee while we saved up to buy a home of our own. We would be staying in Neil's childhood bedroom as his parents wanted to retain their right to use the master bedroom on their occasional visits to the city. And the third bedroom would be the nursery for the baby we hoped to have soon.

Here's the problem. Neil's room had a single twin bed, which would clearly not suffice. A trip to Bloomingdale's to remedy the situation was set up. I cannot for the life of me explain why Neil's mother accompanied us on this errand, but she did. Neil and I had discussed the choice ahead of time and decided to purchase a king-sized bed similar to the one we'd had in Arlington, but more luxurious. Neil's mom started lobbying for two twin beds pushed together with a single headboard. It was good enough for her and her husband. It was good enough for her other sons. This was definitely what was called for!

Neil was now in the middle between his strong-willed mother and his new bride. I took him aside and quietly reminded him of our joint decision. He took a deep breath. "We have decided on the king," he told his mother and the salesman. Nice save!

We lived in Jackson Heights for four years. Michael was conceived in our new bed early that summer and I brought him into the bed to nurse frequently during the nights. Two years later, our second son Will joined our growing family. In 1971, the four of us moved to a home of our own in Westbury, Long Island.

We were accompanied on that journey by our king-sized bed.

"My Next Husband Will Be Normal"

When Neil and I were married, he was very conventional looking. In fact, he could have earned a role in the *Book of Mormon* with his clean-cut good looks and short hair. By the early seventies his look had changed. First he grew sideburns or "mutton chops," then he stopped getting his hair cut, and finally he stopped shaving and grew a beard and mustache. He liked what he saw in the mirror and the fact that it annoyed his oldest brother no end just added to the appeal.

His new look provided a sort of Rorschach test. Some people likened him to Charlie Manson and edged away uneasily. He reminded others of Grizzly Adams and they were drawn to him. At the swimming pool at the Turnberry Isle resort one year, some teenage girls asked the pool attendant if he was Jerry Garcia from the Grateful Dead (he told them yes and they giggled excitedly). Not a few people likened him to Jesus. In fact, when one of Neil's co-workers and close friends was going through a photo album with his young daughter, she pointed to Neil and identified him firmly as "God."

Neil's hair is mostly white now and much longer than mine, and his beard and mustache have that salt and pepper look, while, oddly, his eyebrows remain almost as dark as the day we married. I'm fine with his appearance, especially since he started wearing his hair in a ponytail. But I'm aware that he stands out in a crowd while I do not. I am the vanilla to his "Cherry Garcia."

Years ago I bought a t-shirt from a catalogue with the message "My Next Husband Will Be Normal." Neil wasn't particularly amused but I loved wearing it and it caught the eye of many women we came in contact with. One waitress on a cross-country trip tried to buy it right off my back. Then on an anniversary vacation to Paradise Island in the Bahamas, we went into Nassau to do some shopping. The cashier gave me a strange look and asked, "What's wrong with this one?" I had no idea what she was talking about until she gestured to my t-shirt and repeated her question in an annoyed tone of voice. I mumbled something in reply and retired the shirt shortly afterward.

Today my old t-shirt has a new life in San Diego, where my brother's wife Elisabeth wears it with a gleam in her eye. She even lent it to a neighbor recently to wear to a July 4th barbecue at the home of her neighbor's ex-husband. It was a hit and sparked some lively repartee. We may have started a new trend. The sisterhood of the traveling t-shirt.

Melting Pots

To the best of my knowledge, I was the first member of the Mack family to marry someone Jewish. Interfaith marriage was pretty uncommon in 1967. Now, a mere 45 years later, another Mack has married a member of the Jewish faith. This time it was my nephew Tyler, my brother Warren's son, marrying the love of his life, Ivy Siegel. It was a joyous event, one of those days when everything just comes together, the stars perfectly aligned. The weather was ideal, the bride gorgeous, the mood festive. The guests were a mixture of ages, religions and ethnicities, joined together by their mutual affection for the beaming couple. As my brother so eloquently put it at the rehearsal dinner the evening before, a marriage is more than the uniting of a couple. It is also the blending of two families, in this case, two very different families.

America has been known for centuries as a "melting pot," a mixture of cultures and races and religions. But it wasn't until recent years that inter-marriage became common. Even neighborhoods were frequently Italian, or Polish or Jewish, or even WASP (think Connecticut). I know people my age that grew up literally not knowing anyone outside their own ethnic group. Jews who knew no gentiles; Italians who considered even the Irish as "foreigners." When a Jewish child married outside the faith, parents frequently "sat shiva," in effect declaring their child dead to them. This may still go on in some places, but most of the people I know are just happy nowadays when their child finds someone to love, regardless of their religious or ethnic background.

Tyler and Ivy at their 2012 wedding

Things have definitely changed, some would say for the worse. Personally, as we become a true melting pot, I think American life has greatly improved. When Neil and I married in 1967, it was a bit of a shock to both our families. Neil's older brothers had each married Jewish women (as had virtually all of his cousins), and I was the first in my family to marry a non-Christian. There was a great hue and cry on both sides before our wedding, but fortunately, it settled down nicely by our wedding day. Shortly afterward, Neil's best friend Ron married a Chinese-American, our beloved friend Mai Mai. Several years later my brother Chris married Jenny, a lovely Chinese woman from Indonesia. And mixed marriages of all types have become extremely common in our children's generation.

Through the blending of two families, we learn to cherish one another, not because of our commonalities, but because each side brings something new into the equation. Different perspectives and experiences. Different foods and traditions. And what could be more American than that, a melting pot in the truest sense of the words?

Love As a Four-Letter Word

I was not brought up in household where the word love was used often. Maybe someone would occasionally say, "I love pizza," but I don't remember ever hearing the words "I love you" spoken out loud. They just weren't.

When my parents moved from a house into an assisted living facility in 1993, they had to drastically downsize their possessions. Each of us was given a cardboard box with our name on it containing photos, report cards, letters, etc. Pieces of our childhood carefully saved for posterity. I'd go through my box from time to time, its contents conjuring up the distant past. The letters I wrote home from American University were particularly interesting as they contained many details from everyday campus life that I had forgotten over the years. I was part of the crowd lining Pennsylvania Avenue for Lyndon Johnson's Inauguration parade. Really?

One item in my "memory box" grabbed hold of me. It was a handwritten Mother's Day card that I had given my mom. The penmanship was very childish, so I was probably quite young when I created it. This card and all the box's contents were lost when our house was destroyed by fire in 2009, but I remember the words on this card by heart. Next to a carefully hand-drawn heart were the words "Happy Mother's Day. I love you." Inside were the words, a plea actually: "I hope you love me, too." I wish I could remember a response, a reassuring hug, an "Of course I love you," but I don't. "Love" was a four-letter word. And four-letter words were deemed inappropriate in our household.

How curious that when I married, I chose a man who is equally uncomfortable with saying the words "I love you" aloud. In forty-five years of marriage, I could probably count on one hand the number of times he has told me he loves me. He mocks people we know who end every phone call with a family member, usually a spouse or child, with the words "Love you." I bite my tongue each time, wanting to cry out that, even if said by rote, it is never wrong to tell someone you care about that you love them. What's the downside? That the person who hears the words will feel cherished and a little better about himself as he goes through his day? That sounds like a pretty good deal to me. I know Neil loves me, can't live without me, has my back, etc. But sometimes I just need to hear the words. Just like the little girl on that long ago Mother's Day.

If I were to be asked for one piece of advice to newlyweds, it would be this.

Tell each other every day that you love them. Then prove it through your actions. Love is not a four-letter word. It is the most powerful word in the English language.

Losses

Loss is the necessary counterpart to love. The pain of loss is usually associated with people we love, but it can also apply to an inanimate article, too. When we fought a legal battle in my community to prevent the closure of our local elementary school, I wore my grandmother's wedding ring to court every day. Touching it, twisting it, gave me enormous comfort and calmed me. About the same time that we lost the case, the ring disappeared and I was inconsolable. I wasn't grieving for the ring itself but for what it represented, a connection to my past and a person who had played such a central role in my early years.

I always say there is a rock and roll song for everything in life. Simon and Garfunkle's "I Am a Rock" perfectly describes the connection between love and loss. Every line speaks volumes. "If I never loved I never would have cried. I touch no one and no one touches me."

Total Loss

It's usually a phone call. Not always, but more often than not, it starts with a phone call. Information is delivered and your life becomes permanently reordered into before and after.

The call came on an ordinary November evening in 1967. My best friend's husband asked to speak to my husband. How odd, I thought. The conversation was short and one-sided. When he hung up, my husband relayed the news as gently as possible. Kathy was dead. Her husband had found her in the garage when he came home from work. Asphyxiation. Carbon-monoxide poisoning.

Time stopped. Words lost their meaning. My mind tried to wrap itself around the news but failed. I knew she wasn't happy, but I had no idea of the depth of her despair. In retrospect, I can see that she found herself trapped in a life of dead ends, living someone else's life, and her response was to end it. My major recollection of this period is one of overwhelming numbness. We went to the funeral. I picked out some drawings of Kathy's to remember her by. They were beautiful pencil sketches of her favorite horses, Carry Back and War Admiral. We met with the widower who showed us the note she had left behind. Life went on. Eventually, the numbness wore off leaving deep sorrow and everlasting regret in its wake.

Forty-two years later, my cell phone rang. It was a glorious August afternoon and I was antique shopping in Damariscotta, Maine, while my husband played golf nearby. "Has anyone reached you yet?" asked the voice on the other end. Instantly, my brain kicked into numbness mode. "Your house burned down last night. Here's the number of the police station. They are awaiting your call." Details emerged slowly through a series of phone calls. There was a big storm around midnight, the same storm that downed over 100 trees in Manhattan's Central Park. A large tree on our property had split in half, severing electrical power lines that then landed on the roof of the garage, igniting it. The fire reportedly burned out of control for more than two hours. The entire roof had collapsed and every windowpane in the house was broken.

We returned to our home on Long Island the following day. The home where we had lived for thirty-two years. The home where we had raised our two sons and entertained friends and family. We were warned, but nothing prepares you for the sight of the smoldering corpse of your family home. It was heartbreaking.

"Total loss," declared the insurance agent on the scene. We were able to scavenge a few items. Our unused tickets to Woodstock. Some porcelain planters. A mirror bought at auction when the estate next door was sold. Miraculously, the two tropical fish in the living room had lived through the blaze. They accompanied us to a nearby hotel in Glen Cove that night. This little triumph pleased my husband no end. But the den attached to the garage was literally gone. There was nothing left to board up. All the mementos and photo albums I cherished had gone up in smoke. Kathy's drawings, so carefully preserved through the years, were gone. It was as if they had never existed.

Life went on. The house was rebuilt and it is spectacular. Friends and family came by to see it last summer. Several made jokes about burning down their own homes so they, too, could build new ones. I faked amusement. Because the floor plan of the new house is identical, I can enter the new den and stare at the wall, now bare, where Kathy's drawings once hung. I see them in my mind's eye. They will exist as long as I am around to remember them.

"Total loss," said the insurance agent. "Total loss," I whisper to myself.

The Gift

The death of a parent is always hard, but if you are very lucky, it can be a good death.

As recently as 1993, Neil and I had both sets of our parents. By 2007, we were down to just my mother, Ruth. Improbably, given her two bouts with breast cancer at a relatively early age, my mother lived to be the oldest of our four parents.

The beginning of the end was a routine visit to her doctor in August of 2007. She entered the office complaining of allergies and some shortness of breath. After a chest X-ray, she left the office with a diagnosis of lung cancer. Her reaction was one of shock and anger, as she had never smoked during any of her 88 years.

When she called us with the news, Neil and I left New York hurriedly to be with her for moral support when she met with an oncologist near her assisted living facility. She entered the examining room clad in the usual ridiculous paper gown, but with her double strand of pearls around her neck, earrings in place, makeup just so. The cancer was well advanced (stage four) the doctor informed us, and the options were few. There were some trials going on in another part of the state which he could try to get her enrolled in if she so desired. My mother made her decision quickly and decisively. There would be no heroic efforts or chemotherapy for her. She would go home and continue to live her life as before. She was given a prognosis of six months.

My sister Marci, the eldest and therefore most responsible of us four children, quickly rearranged her life to move from Vermont to

North Carolina, where my parents had retired to in 1980. She set up an office in my mom's apartment so she could do her accounting job by computer. I spent the next six months shuttling back and forth to my mom's from our Florida condo, a ten-hour drive made easier by the Beatles tunes on my CD player. A hospice team was assembled and the kindness of each of its members was incredibly comforting.

"What do you do for fun?" asked the hospice medical director on one visit in my mom's living room. "We have lots of fun," Mom replied breezily. "We do crossword puzzles, watch DVDs and never miss *Dancing with the Stars*. And we laugh a lot." She insisted that this time be "just the Mack girls." No men allowed, which hurt my husband's feelings as he and my mom had become very close through the years. Whenever she kissed me goodbye as I headed home to Florida, she would always add, "Please thank Neil for letting you come."

The last Christmas was bittersweet but never maudlin. She directed the placement of all the holiday decorations around her apartment, Marci's job. She told me what homemade treats to prepare to be handed out to friends and staff members. Marci called me once as I was making several pounds of candied pecans in my Florida kitchen. Instead of my usual rather haphazard placement on the cookie sheets, I was obsessively lining them up in neat little rows, all right side up, as if by making them "perfect" I could delay the inevitable.

In February, my brothers and sisters-in-law were summoned from their homes in California and Arizona, as it appeared the end was approaching. There were no tears, at least in front of my mom, and she was so thrilled to have us all together again one last time.

We celebrated mom's 89th birthday on March 12th. She barely touched the chocolate birthday cake, but spoke animatedly on the phone with my brother Chris, describing in detail every flower in the lovely arrangement he and Jenny had sent. Mom died five days later, almost six months to the day after her diagnosis.

Those final months had been her gift to us. Thanks to her decisions to forgo chemo and engage the services of hospice, we never had to watch her suffer. Thanks to us, and Marci in particular, she never had to spend her final months alone. Instead, she spent those months surrounded by loving friends and family members.

Especially, "the Mack girls."

The Mack girls in a photo taken by Marla, a hospice nurse

The Brookville School, R.I.P.

When we began searching for our dream house in 1976, we bought a home on Pine Valley Road, subject to an engineer's inspection. Neil and I visited the local elementary school serviced by that house, the Brookville School, and fell in love with it. We felt that its small size, one class per grade, would be ideal for our sons. When the engineer's report came back citing serious flaws, we withdrew our offer and began to search for another home served by the Brookville School. Luckily, we found a house just blocks away and moved in the following January, right around the time of our tenth wedding anniversary.

The transition went smoothly. Even though the boys entered mid-year, they felt at home there right from the start. We settled in and expected to have many years before we had to worry about the problems they would face in a larger school setting. Within two years, there was talk in the school district about closing the Brookville School permanently and selling the land. When the school had been incorporated into the adjoining Locust Valley School District many years earlier, there had been a gentleman's agreement that the Brookville School would remain open indefinitely in return for the generous tax dollars the area's homeowners would be contributing. It turns out that "gentleman's agreements" aren't worth anything in a court of law, which is where the dispute finally ended up.

Despite all our best efforts, the school closed shortly after the court ruled that it was within the school board's purview to do so. The building was used as a community center for several years until the district finally sold the land to a developer for a pittance. Before long, the school simply disappeared from the landscape, replaced by several large homes with spacious grounds. When the Brookville School closed, some parents enrolled their children in private schools, but the majority of us sent our children to the elementary schools in Locust Valley. Mike and Will adjusted, as children do, better than we did. But it wasn't the same. The Intermediate School in Locust Valley is a large, three-story structure, presenting difficulties for children with physical disabilities. After Will had corrective knee surgery when he was ten, he couldn't negotiate the many steps to get to the lower floor for a science class. So he missed out.

Life in the neighborhood changed, too. Since we have no downtown or public areas, the school had been the hub that the community revolved around. Even long after their children had outgrown the school, residents would attend school events there. There is no gathering place now. No place to meet the neighbors.

The Brookville School is just a distant memory now. Of better times, times when "gentlemen" lived up to their promises.

The Smartest Man in the Room

Michael Harrington was a genius. He was also the best professor I ever had.

True to his populist beliefs, this learned man chose to teach at Queens College in Flushing, NY. He would have been a welcome addition to the faculty of Harvard or Yale or Princeton or any of the "Ivies," but instead he chose to teach at a public university. I found myself a few credits short of my degree in political science in 1983, so I signed up for his class on a whim. I was vaguely aware of his pedigree. His book, *The Other America,* had been greatly influential in the Kennedy and Johnson administrations, informing the country's War on Poverty. A college graduate at just nineteen, Michael Harrington was considered to be the country's leading Democratic Socialist, an effective debater, and an intellectual in the truest sense of the word.

I was surprised when he showed up for the first class in faded blue jeans, looking more like a student than a professor. From the time he began to speak, I was in awe. My hands flew across the pages of my notebook, trying to put down every word for posterity. He gave the class a new way of looking at society, a unique perspective all his own. One young student tried to argue policy with him, unaware that he was totally over his head. "Shut up," I wanted to say him. "Shut up and learn from the master. Stop wasting precious time."

Five years later, I read in the *New York Times* about a planned tribute to Professor Harrington, to be held in the Roseland Ballroom in Manhattan. He was in the latter stages of cancer of the esophagus at the time, and his friends and admirers wisely decided to pay him tribute before rather than after his death. I bought two tickets to the affair and drove into the city with Neil, who was curious about this professor I had been talking about through the years. Roseland was packed with more than 600 people. We sat through an endless series of speeches, each more boring than the last. Finally, he was introduced to the crowd by feminist icon Gloria Steinem, who was warm and witty and thoroughly engaging.

At long last, the man himself stood at the podium, his voice strong, clearly feeding off the energy of the crowd. There he was, my brilliant, mesmerizing professor, rising to the occasion, proving that he was still the smartest man in the room. He sent our spirits soaring. Afterward, Neil turned to me with tears in his eyes. "Wow," he exclaimed. He got it. Some people really are bigger than life, and if we are really, really lucky, we get to share time and space with them.

Michael Harrington died the following year at the age of sixty-one. Gone too soon, but how lucky was I to have been a part of his world?

Momma Nancy

They say it takes a village to raise a child. I was lucky enough to have not one but two mothers who raised me.

Momma Nancy became a fixture in my life during my adolescence. In the late 1950s, I was hired to baby-sit her daughters. First it was just Susan and Sande, and later, the baby, Betsy. Nancy introduced me to another way to live. She was beautiful, but it was her vivaciousness and love of life that drew me to her. She taught me about mothering, and fashion, and decorating. She taught me about life.

When she was diagnosed with late-stage ovarian cancer in 1982 at the age of fifty-two, Nancy characteristically threw herself into the battle. She was not going down without a fight! She enrolled in a pilot program for ovarian cancer at the National Institutes of Health that also included the wife of the Chief Justice of the Supreme Court. She managed to obtain every trial drug as it came on the market. She would not take "no" for an answer. She appeared on ABC's *20/20*, vowing to win her battle against the disease. In between treatments, she lived her life fully, traveling to Europe, going on a whale watch, cherishing her two grandsons as well as her three grown daughters.

During one visit to her in Boca Raton, Nancy and I went to a flea market, where she bought a number of watches, more than anyone could possibly need, as if trying to buy time, for herself, for all those she loved. I think it was around that time that I sensed that she would not be with us for long. So I put pen to paper and wrote a tribute to her, about what she had meant to me and how knowing her had enriched my life. I sent the published piece to her for Mother's Day, and she had it framed and placed it in a prominent place in her kitchen.

Sadly, after an eight-year fight, ovarian cancer won the battle. She called me one day. "Paul," she said (she was the only person who ever called me Paul). "I'm terminal." The words sent chills up my spine and I rushed to Boca to see her one last time. Her husband George met me outside to prepare me for Nancy's condition. But, of course, nothing could prepare me for the sight of the frail old lady who struggled to get to her feet to greet me. Cancer had robbed Nancy of her beauty, her vitality, even her appetite as she picked at her food during lunch. She was only sixty, but she looked many decades older.

I cried all the way home to Aventura. George told me later that she cried too after our final meeting, telling him tearfully, "I'll never see Paul again." She entered hospice care and died soon afterward. I spoke at her funeral, but I have no recollection of what I said. I felt bereft and still do twenty years later. What I wouldn't give to hear her voice once again, calling me "Paul."

The Anne Frank House

I won a free trip for two to Europe at a charity raffle in 1984, and we immediately made plans to visit a number of European cities. The flight was to and from Paris on Air France, so we bought Eurail passes ahead of time and made reservations for hotels in the Netherlands, Germany and southern France. Amsterdam was on the itinerary, and while there we decided to visit the Anne Frank House, now a museum. When we entered the house and started the long climb up those steep stairs, I started to sob. Neil looked at me quizzically, then wisely let me be. I cried my way through the entire tour. I cried for the young girl who had written her diary within those walls, never knowing it would someday be published and make her famous. I cried for her lost innocence and my own.

When I was eleven, my Girl Scout troop went to see a theater production of *The Diary of Anne Frank*. I had not read the book yet, so the storyline was unknown to me. I was totally unprepared for the play's ending. I left the theater in a state of shock. There were people in the world so evil that they would think nothing of killing a young girl like Anne Frank, a young girl like me. I tried not to dwell on it, but for years I heard the police sirens in my dreams and had nightmares about the S.S. troops coming to find me.

It took a trip to Anne Frank's house to bring it all back to me. The recognition that there really are evil people in the world. People who wish harm, even to children. Children like Anne Frank. Children like me.

Little Boy Lost

Following the death of my father-in-law in 1998, we unearthed a remarkable photo of Neil taken at about three years of age, his adorable face surrounded by a cascade of long dark curls. He has a somewhat wary look on his face, as if he could see into the future. The picture was taken shortly before he had a "before and after" moment which would change his life forever.

Neil was the third child in his family, born following his mother's two miscarriages. His brothers were eight and twelve when he arrived, and served more as uncles to him than brothers. He was the light of his mother's life and she took him with her everywhere. They went shopping together. He played on the floor with toy cars while she played mah jongg with her friends. When she cooked or gossiped with the neighbors, he was always within earshot. They were, in short, inseparable, and he felt safe and secure and beloved.

Everything changed the year he turned four. His father decided without warning that it was time to separate mother and child, and plans were made to send Neil to school. It wasn't a neighborhood school. It was a yeshiva, many miles from home, which he attended from early morning until suppertime. He has a clear memory of his mother running after the station wagon taking him away from home on his first day of school while he was crying hysterically inside. He adjusted to the situation but he learned some hard lessons that day. About trust, about families, his own, in particular.

Naturally, we raised our sons very differently, gradually introducing them to the outside world. First play dates, then play groups, followed by nursery school for short periods of time. They grew up to be trusting children, unlike their father, who had real issues with trust until well into adulthood.

I look at that photo of that precious little boy and think of how different his life would have been, should have been, had he not been robbed of his childhood innocence at the age of four.

Remembering Lenice

Charm has been defined as the ability of someone to make you think both of you are pretty wonderful. My friend Lenice was charming by this or any other definition. Lenice exuded charm and an enthusiasm for life that made you relish being in her company. She was as unique as her name.

We met at the Brookville School in 1977, where her two youngest children were in the same grades as my two sons. The following year, I worked with Lenice to prevent the school board from closing that school, a fight we lost but one that drew us and the rest of the community at large closer. During the years that followed, Lenice's presence was everywhere. She was on the Locust Valley School Board, the Upper Brookville Board of Trustees, and finally, served as the first female mayor of Upper Brookville. In the latter capacity, she described meeting former President Bill Clinton, who peppered her with questions about what it was like to be the mayor of a small village. I have no doubt that Lenice charmed him, too.

The former Brookville School Council still meets monthly, even though the school closed more than thirty years ago. We call it "Ladies Who Lunch" now, poking gentle fun at ourselves. When I'm in New York, it's my job to organize these get-togethers, and Lenice was always my first call. She was the center of attention, not because she was the mayor, but because she was always the life of the party. She greeted everyone with a big hug and warm kiss. She charmed us with her stories and bawdy jokes, told with that distinctive Welsh accent of hers.

My husband is notoriously reluctant about socializing, but Neil and I had a rare dinner out with Lenice and her husband Herman shortly before leaving for Florida in 2008. She ate with relish and regaled us with stories, and, in general, gave no hint of what lay just around the corner. Shortly after we arrived in Aventura, I received an e-mail from Lenice, saying she had just been diagnosed with acute leukemia. She vowed to fight it with all her resources. It would be her last e-mail. Tragically, she lost her fight just two months later. She left behind a bereft husband, four children, four grandchildren and many, many dear neighbors and friends, all of whom miss her terribly.

We "ladies" still get together for lunch on a monthly basis, but it just isn't the same without our Lenice.

Fearless Polly and the Brookville Cop

Each time a friend or neighbor dies, a little part of us dies with them. So to get through the pain, we focus on fond memories.

I knew my friend and neighbor of thirty-plus years was in failing health. But when I received three e-mails all with the subject line "Polly," I opened them with a heavy heart. We were still in Florida so I missed the memorial service although I was there in spirit.

The thing that made Polly such a unique person was her fearlessness. She didn't care what others thought. She made her own rules as she went through life. Her family was her greatest priority: her husband Palmer, her three sons, and the many grandchildren who enriched their lives. When Palmer died in 2005, much too young at sixty-nine, Polly threw a wonderful party in their backyard where neighbors chatted beside the lovely pond and dined on sumptuous foods. The memorial service in the nearby Brookville Reformed Church earlier that day had been a wonderful tribute to Palmer with warm personal stories and live folk music, a fitting sendoff.

My favorite Polly story, which I have told numerous times through the years, concerned Polly driving down Wolver Hollow Road above the posted village speed limit of 35 mph. Our area is patrolled by the Old Brookville Police Department, a private force, and the area residents essentially are their employers. So when a local resident is stopped, they are rarely ticketed. I was stopped for speeding once on nearby Route 106, and after showing the proper contrition and promising to slow down in the future, I was sent on my merry way. But that was not Polly's way. The police officer explained to Polly that he'd been asked by her fellow residents on Wolver Hollow Road to stop cars that were speeding down the street, making it unsafe. "I'll let you go with a warning if you promise me you won't do this again," he told her. "Well then just write me the ticket now," she replied. "I'm not going to make a promise I know I won't keep." The poor cop was speechless for a moment and then let her go with a feeble request that she just *try* not to speed again. Pure Polly!

How we miss our old friend.

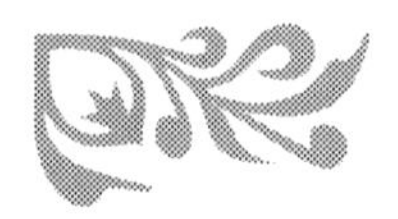

It Is What It Is

The 5 am phone call woke us both up in our New Orleans hotel room. True to form for a call at such an ungodly hour, the news was not good. There had been a traffic accident in lower Manhattan several hours earlier. Our niece Judith was dead. Her father, my husband's brother, was in critical condition. It was the final day of the 2004 annual Mack family reunion and I went about the day's activities in a daze. Here we were in the city Judith had called home for the four years she attended Tulane University, while she laid in a morgue in New York City.

Details emerged. A chronic drunk driver had plowed into the passenger side of their car, killing Judith instantly. Her heart had literally burst from the impact. They had been crossing an intersection on Grand Street on the way to work at Fulton Fish Market when a drunken party planner went through a red light on a side street, sending their car hurtling into the air, ultimately landing on a fence. The driver, who had a blood alcohol level of .27 (three times the legal limit) was unhurt and tried to flee the scene. Only in Manhattan could you find witnesses at three a.m. They held him down until the police arrived. The following year he was convicted of second-degree murder and vehicular manslaughter. The case drew an enormous amount of publicity and was the focus of a story on NBC's *Dateline.*

But the reality of that day was that Judith, the 37-year-old mother of three young sons, beloved wife of a doctor, and only daughter of her parents, was gone. I called a month later to see how my sister-in-law was coping with the loss. Unexpectedly, Judith's husband picked up the phone. "How are you doing?" I blurted out without thinking. "It is what it is," he replied, which I thought was an odd choice of words. I've heard those exact words many times since, about situations both trivial and profound. It seemed cold-hearted to me at first, but in retrospect, the words seem fitting. Here was a man left to raise his three sons without his wife, all because a party planner chose to drink himself into a stupor and then drive himself home. You could rail all you wanted against the culprit, but the bottom line was that everyone involved had to adjust to the new reality. Nothing would bring back Judith. Nothing.

"It is what it is," stated the new widower.

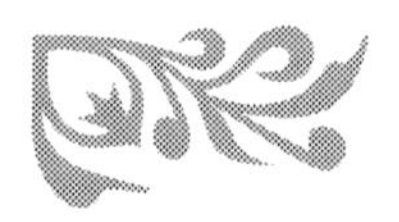 

Libby, the Un-Beige

In a sizeable condo like ours, most people just blend into the larger group, kind of like beige. Others are unique. They stand out. They are the red in a sea of beige.

Libby Charles had a personality that was a vibrant red, and she called Mystic Pointe Tower 300 her home for the last twenty years of her long life. Her real name was Lillian, but everyone called her Libby. She was one of the first residents here and she was a character in the best sense of the word. She always told it like it was. There would be no sugar coating it for Libby. Other people whispered about a staff member who claimed to be "straight." "He's gay," declared Libby. "Any man who mentions his wife in every other sentence has got to be gay." There was no fooling Libby.

Libby would have made a terrific character actress or comedian. But when she was widowed at just thirty-five with two young sons to support, she went to work for the Social Security Administration in her beloved Baltimore. She nurtured creativity in her sons and later appeared in commercials for her son Allan, who worked in advertising and public relations. Her other son was known as "Stan the Fan" and he hosted a radio talk show about sports with a popular segment called *Beat My Mom.* Guess who played the mom as fans tried to compete with her in guessing sports outcomes? And guess who usually came out on top?

She was inordinately and justifiably proud of her grandson, Josh Charles, the actor. I'm a big fan of his and once rode the elevator with him at our condo, he looking cool behind his designer sunglasses, me trying my best not to stare or blurt out something inane. His breakout role was in the movie, *Dead Poets Society*, but in more recent years Josh has starred in numerous television series, including the cult classic, *Sports Night*, and HBO's *In Treatment*. Libby died before Josh's latest starring role as Will in *The Good Wife*. She would have greatly enjoyed his success in this popular show, and gotten an enormous kick out of his being named this year to *People* magazine's list of "The Sexiest Men Alive."

Libby died of heart failure in 2008 at the age of eighty-five. Condo life goes on, as it inevitably does, but it is a little less colorful now. A little more beige.

Thinking Thin

Jody and I have been good friends for more than thirty-five years. She spotted me at a parents meeting at the Brookville School in 1977. As a new resident to the area, I must have been looking a bit lost, so Jody invited me over for a cup of coffee afterward. That simple act of kindness led to many years of close friendship. It turned out that our properties practically abutted one another in a catty-cornered way. In those days, there were no fences between properties, and a well-worn path soon developed linking her yard to mine.

We have both had more than our share of triumphs and tragedies in the years since. Neil and I were there as each of Jody and Ed's four children walked down the aisle. I mourned with her when they lost an infant granddaughter to a rare neurological disorder, and shared her grief when her beautiful daughter Lori died in a car accident on the Garden State Parkway.

But over the years, one thing remained the same for the two of us: thinking thin. Every Thursday morning, Jody and I would go to the local chapter of "Think Thin" in Glen Cove, and then we'd head to the Old Brookville Diner for a bite to eat and a heart-to-heart chat. It was the one constant in our lives. We "thought thin" but rarely lost weight. When my mother met Jody, she exclaimed, "You look like sisters!" We weren't, of course, but we did form our own kind of sisterhood.

Jody and Ed moved farther east on Long Island five years ago, just far enough away to make frequent get-togethers too difficult to manage. It has been several years since I've seen Jody in person, but we do keep in touch through the occasional e-mail and on Face-book. The path between our houses has grown over, and the Old Brookville Diner has been replaced by a commercial bank. But I still think of Jody often and miss seeing her on a regular basis.

There will always be a special place in my heart for my "sister" Jody.

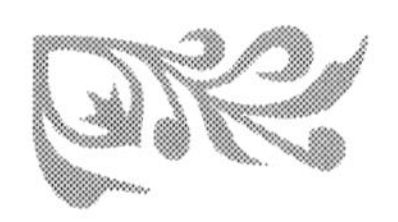

Candle in the Wind

Marilyn Monroe has always fascinated me. Watching her perform in movies as I grew up, I thought she exuded sensuality and mystery. She was a ball of contradictions. Playful, yet sexy. Girlish, but with a very womanly body. The men she married were as varied as her personas. What did Joe DiMaggio and Arthur Miller have in common other than having been married to her?

You rarely think about the person behind the icon, but I read an article published in *Life* magazine shortly before her death in 1962. She made an open, desperate plea to be taken seriously. To not be regarded as a "joke." It moved me tremendously and made me consider her in a different light. I realized for the first time how insecure she was, how unaware she was of her tremendous talent and unique ability to steal any scene she appeared in. It also made me realize the power of journalism to enlighten the reader. When she died only weeks later, I grieved for the "real" Marilyn, the one who had begged to be taken seriously. She didn't live to see the women's movement come of age later in that decade, ushering in a new era when women demanded respect and a seat at the table.

It wasn't until more than ten years later that Elton John wrote his beautiful tribute to her, "Candle in the Wind." What a wonderful metaphor for this insecure and fragile human being. She was arguably the most famous woman in the world at the time of her death, but she died alone, oblivious to the effect her life and death would have on millions of people for many, many years to come.

Guilty

When asked the inevitable question about what sex they prefer, the automatic answer of every mother-to-be is invariably, "It doesn't matter, as long as it's healthy." It's the knee-jerk response, the politically correct answer. But what if the baby isn't healthy? What then?

The thing about raising a handicapped child is that the parents are usually not. So when the child develops differently from his peers and his parents, the parents have no road map, no compass to guide them. They can respond in one of two ways. They can focus on the "normal" features of the child, or throw themselves into fixing the "defects," as a form letter from our school district so indelicately put it until I pointed out its inappropriateness.

I chose the first option. I spent the early years of my sons' lives concentrating on the "normal." At some point, I was chosen to participate in a television show as the token "model" parent of a handicapped child. I remember pleading earnestly with the studio audience, "I want people to see the child first instead of the handicap." And that's the way we dealt with the situation, my two handicapped sons and their parents.

When he was two, our oldest son Michael was diagnosed with cerebral palsy. He had met all the other age-appropriate milestones for his age but never got out of the "toddling" stage. He was bright and adorable, a cheerful little boy who was easy to love. I was so charmed by his many assets that it never occurred to me that everyone else wouldn't succumb as well.

And then came reality in a series of rude awakenings. There was a playgroup mother who asked that Michael stay home when it was her turn to host the group. A nursery school director who claimed his staff would quit "en masse" if he allowed a "child like that" to enroll in his school. A sister-in-law who stopped inviting him to his cousin's birthday parties after his handicap became more apparent. He scared the other children, she claimed. I absorbed the blows, protected my child and went forward. I was so intent on ignoring the handicap that when we lost Michael briefly at Jones Beach one summer, my frantic description was "three years old, red bathing suit, curly brown hair." "Oh," replied the lifeguard. "You mean the crippled kid." We were quickly reunited but his words remained in the air. "The crippled kid..."

When Mike was two, his brother Will arrived on the scene. It was shortly before Mike's diagnosis, and for one brief shining moment, I was the mother of two "perfect" babies. A harried, happy, stay-at-home mom, who was content with the world. Then came the diagnosis. Cerebral palsy, most likely due to the umbilical cord having been wrapped around his neck at birth. Okay, but he was still adorable and bright and Will was fine. Until two years later when it became apparent that Will too, would not be getting out of the "toddling" stage. I mentioned my fears to Mike's orthopedist, who dismissed them out of hand. When he examined Will again several months later, he changed his mind, agreeing that my fears were justified. It was one of the only times in my life that I wanted to be wrong. Cerebral palsy was again the diagnosis, milder this time, but still...

How did this happen? I had tried so hard to be the perfect mother-to-be. I had "normal" pregnancies during which I refused to take even an aspirin. I breastfed my babies, long before nursing became fashionable. I was the quintessential "earth mother." What had gone wrong? Like other parents of children with handicaps, I grieved for what might have been. The loss of those "perfect children" I had dreamed about since my own childhood.

The years went by. The boys enrolled in public schools on Long Island. It was the early days of mainstreaming, so "special" schools were never under consideration. Nor were any of the fancy private schools nearby, not after our nightmare experience with the nursery school owner. Both boys had above-average intelligence, so handling the public school curriculum was not a problem for them. I served as a class mother, went on countless field trips and volunteered to serve as a parent member of the awkwardly named "Committee on the Handicapped." The boys and I made weekly trips to the local cerebral palsy center for physical therapy, but otherwise, we concentrated on the "normal." I became an advocate for people with cerebral palsy, overcoming my shyness and taking on speaking assignments in the public schools, pleading for acceptance and understanding for kids who were "different." I told the students: "One thing about cerebral palsy is that it doesn't get worse over time. It isn't progressive." *It's not so bad, I told myself. This is doable. At least it isn't progressive.*

Except it was. When the boys were in their late teens, we were referred to the Institute for Basic Research in Staten Island. They were put through an exhaustive series of tests and observations. We met with a geneticist. We learned that they had a neurological condition far less common than cerebral palsy, one that affects only a handful of children in the country and for which there is no cure. It was a "male only" condition resulting from a defective gene from the mother. At the time, all I could hear was that it was my fault. It was my gene. Mine. The geneticist explained that with each pregnancy, I had a one-in-four chance of having a baby with the defective gene. If we had a daughter, she would have had a fifty-fifty chance of inheriting the "bad" gene, which she could later pass on to her children. We were told that the good news was that a male could not be a carrier, so if the boys had children, they would be "normal."

For once in my life, I failed to focus on the good news. I was devastated by the fact that it was my gene that had caused all the pain and suffering. I never told my mother. She died not knowing it was her gene, passed on to me, that was responsible for the boys' condition. I protected her because I knew how devastated she would have been. After all, the apple doesn't fall far from the tree.

Mike is now 44. He is unable to feed or bathe himself. Luckily, we have a live-in nurse/companion, Heather, who takes care of him as if he were her own child. Mike can speak only with great difficulty, but his mind is still sharp, his sense of humor somehow intact. He is still Mike, trapped inside a body that no longer functions in any "normal" way.

Will is 42 now. He lost his ability to walk in his twenties, and until this year could drive a car using hand controls and live independently. He married when he was 27 and he and his wife had a baby boy the following summer, our grandson Jordan. Now fourteen, Jordan is a miniature version of his father, but without the handicap. He is perfect and I revel in that perfection. And then I feel guilty. I want to go back in time and change the roll of the dice and choose the eggs without the defective gene. And then I feel guilty. I've committed no crime but that doesn't take away the guilt.

"It's okay," whispers my inner ballerina. "You can't help how you feel. But remember to focus on all the many good times in the past, and take each new day as it comes."

Mike and Will, 1972

Family

Families are like tribes. You don't get to choose the family you are born into, and when you marry, it can be difficult to break the code of the new family you are now part of. As a result, the feeling of being an "outsider" may never go away. This didn't happen to me but I know of many people who never broke that code and, as a result, never felt they belonged.

Neil and I each have a sibling who adopted a child. In my sister's case, it was two daughters. Those children were readily accepted into the Mack and Smith tribes without reservation. Though we don't share common bloodlines, they are as much a part of our families as any of the children born into them.

I changed my name to my husband's upon our marriage. It was the custom of the time, but before long, many brides began hyphenating their last names. Now many new brides just keep their maiden names, especially if they have established themselves in their professions. Part of me now regrets the name change because I was born a Mack and will always be a Mack. My compromise was to start using my maiden name as my middle name. It's not a perfect solution but it will have to do.

We Are Family

I can't remember the exact date of our first Mack family reunion, but let's just say that my immediate family began holding annual reunions at least several decades ago. My mother would begin planning these get-togethers months in advance and reunion photos would appear prominently in the calendars she made as holiday gifts each year. Because we were so spread out geographically, the reunions would often be the only time my siblings and I would see one another. My mom would always foot the bill, calling it "spending your inheritance."

The locations would vary. Frequently, the reunion would be held on Long Island near us. Once it was held on Lake Champlain near Marci's home in Burlington, Vermont. Twice we met in San Diego near my brother Warren's home with a side trip to Mexico one year, and Las Vegas another. For my parents' fiftieth wedding anniversary, we gathered in Cape Cod at a quaint inn in Orleans, Massachusetts. A really memorable reunion was held in New Orleans, the year before Katrina devastated the city. And several times we met in Florida at or near our Aventura condo. The final reunions were in North Carolina, as my mother found traveling long distances tiring and stressful in her later years. So we would gather near her retirement home in the Carolina Foothills for her convenience. Our last reunion was at a hotel on Lake Lure, a beautiful setting where meals were included.

Our gatherings were always boisterous, featuring fiercely competitive games of Scrabble and basketball and tennis, even croquet on at least one occasion. Food was also a major factor and finding restaurants to accommodate all of us was sometimes a real challenge. It often seemed like all we did was eat, planning the next meal as soon as one was done. And when my mom went to sleep, the "boys" would inevitably head for the nearest pizzeria for a late night snack.

The other feature of our reunions was the Chinese auction. (I have no idea why it was called that.) We would bring wrapped items varying wildly in value, and draw numbers. Family members would open their prizes to laughter or sighs of envy. The rules changed from year to year and sometimes you could "steal" someone else's treasure. I always included special gifts for the youngest family members, which were off limits to the adults. Chris and Warren would bring items from their overseas travels, my sister-in-law Jenny would bring her beautiful hand crafted jewelry, and Marci brought "treasures" from garage sales and some Vermont specialties. Political items were my department and always a big hit, from the Nixon t-shirt ("He's tanned, He's ready...") to an Everett Dirksen album, which reappeared every few years, and a Dan Quayle autobiography that nobody wanted. Funny hats were also a huge hit for some reason. The hands-down most popular item ever was a t-shirt I brought to a Vermont reunion that said, "I survived my dysfunctional family." Luckily, I brought two, so my nephew Tyler and niece Julie each ended up with one.

Back in the late 1960s, my sister and her husband adopted their two daughters after providing them with foster care for several years. During their teenage years, they had some identity issues, which is common among adopted children. They even searched for and found some members of their "real" family at one point. This was a painful subject we didn't discuss much. But I have a very clear memory of a scene from my son Will's wedding in 1997. My nieces were in their late twenties at the time, their identity problems long since resolved. Audrey, the older of the two, excitedly led me to the dance floor. "They are playing a special song I asked for," she told me. It was "We Are Family." My mother overheard this exchange and had tears in her eyes. She wasn't the only one. Memories like this one can't be bought at any price.

Marci with Julie and Audrey

Mom and Emily in North Carolina

Dad and Warren at a Long Island reunion

Warren, me, Mom, Chris and Marci at the 2001 reunion in Florida

In Mackville, Vermont: Neil, me Marci, Mom with Emily, Chris, Jenny and Warren

Last reunion, Lake Lure: Emily, Neil, me, Elisabeth, Warren, Mom, Chris and Jenny

Sunrise, Sunset

There is an old saying that for every death, a child is born. Sometimes, it happens within a family, and the result is a roller coaster of emotions that leaves you with a form of whiplash. Agony and ecstasy. Joy and sorrow. Unspeakable sadness and indescribable elation.

In our household, it happened in July of 1998. Neil's father had been fading fast. Now in his 87th year, the prostate cancer diagnosed three years earlier had apparently returned and spread to his bones. He was determined to die at home in his own bed and on his own terms. It would be our final gift to him. We visited often, crossing the Whitestone Bridge on the hour-long journey to his home in Peekskill. Every week, he grew visibly worse and we made our way home with heavy hearts.

One morning, we received an unexpected call from Florida, informing us that our grandson would be making an early entrance, three weeks before his due date. We threw our hastily packed bags into the trunk of our car and headed south, doing 95 on 95, as we would later tell the story to our grandson, Jordan. We were summoned to the delivery room just minutes after his birth. "Come meet your grandson," said our son Will proudly. We approached him with awe. He was red and splotchy and wrinkled and fabulous, weighing in at a healthy eight pounds despite the early delivery. I began dialing everyone I ever knew on my cell phone with the joyous news.

We spent the next week getting to know the newest member of the Smith and Mack clans. I spent hours memorizing the features of his tiny precious face. I shot a roll of film of just Jordan. Jordan sleeping!

Jordan awake! Jordan yawning! Jordan drinking his bottle! When I went to have the film processed, I ripped open the envelope just outside the photo store's entrance and sat on a bench staring at the pictures. A stranger approached me. "I don't know what you are looking at but you have a look of such joy on your face," she told me. I showed her the photos and she pretended to be impressed.

At week's end, we headed back to New York. I embarrassed Neil by showing the photos of Jordan to every waitress along the I-95 corridor. Instead of heading for Long Island, we went straight to Peekskill to see Neil's dad. I tried to share the news with him and show him the pictures, but he was too ill to appreciate them. He died several weeks later on July 28th, Jordan's due date.

Sunrise, sunset.

An Uncommon Man

When my Uncle Henry died in 2008, the newspapers in Vermont published lengthy obituaries complete with photographs, followed by numerous letters to the editor about him. He was lauded as a "man at peace with the world," "an iconic Burlington character," "a poet who could converse well on anything," and "a man in touch with the natural world." But he was more than those things. He was also a hobo without a train. He was homeless by choice. He led a truly unconventional life.

He was born in 1924, the third and youngest child of my paternal grandparents, Warren Williams Mack and Christabel Brown Mack. His full name was Henry Resolved Mack II. The name Resolved has a long history in our family dating back to the Mayflower, when the first child born in America was an ancestor of ours named Resolved White.

Unlike his older siblings, Uncle Henry had a proclivity for getting into trouble at an early age, despite the fact that his father (my grandfather) was a strict disciplinarian and the State Highway Commissioner of Delaware. Henry was a graduate of St. John's College with degrees in philosophy and literature. During World War II, he was a conscientious objector, which was almost unheard of at the time. My father served as a captain in the army, while Uncle Henry volunteered for alternative service as a medical guinea pig. The army doctors would give him malaria, and then try out cures on him. He later studied theology at Boston University, then switched to social work and earned a master's degree. When his empathy for the clients got in the way of his productivity, he began taking odd jobs as a taxi driver and house painter. He was also quite an artist. I inherited two pencil drawings he made of his two grandmothers, Grandmother Brown and Grandmother Mack. They are incredibly photographic in detail. The portrait of Grandmother Mack is particularly remarkable as Henry was only ten years old when he drew it.

Uncle Henry married twice, first to Doris May, and later to Mildred. He had no children of his own, though Mildred's children from her first marriage remember him fondly. My grandmother would display the photos of Mildred's children along with those of the rest of her grandchildren. This was during the era when interracial marriage was very rare, almost taboo in American society. The fact that they were black, as was Mildred, did not bother my grandmother in the least.

We saw very little of Uncle Henry when we were growing up. In retrospect, the reason may be this. When my youngest brother, Chris, was a preschooler in the mid-1950s, Uncle Henry offered to take him to the Bronx Zoo one day while the rest of us were in school. My parents agreed, never dreaming that Uncle Henry would leave Chris alone at the zoo while he ran some errands. When the zoo closed for the day, poor Chris was asked to leave. He walked tearfully into the gas station across the street, where he was given ice cream and the police were called. Chris rode the police car to the station house where Uncle Henry eventually located him. He begged Chris not to tell my parents of this "adventure" and Chris kept quiet for about a week. He finally broke down and told my parents the whole story. The rest of us didn't learn of it until forty years later when we put together a memory album in honor of my parents' fiftieth wedding anniversary.

Uncle Henry returned to Vermont in the 1970s and made his home in the Burlington area, living a catch-as-catch-can existence. He built a rudimentary shelter for himself out of scrap metal and discarded lumber. His living room was just a chair with an umbrella to protect him from the rain. His stove was a pretzel can. When even this humble abode was destroyed by fire, he took to living on the streets and under train trestles. He rummaged through dumpsters behind stores for food, which he readily shared with others. He redeemed bottles and cans for cash. He made friends easily, especially with the local police. When the weather was especially cold, he would approach a cop and tell him he was about to steal a candy bar and where. The cop would then "arrest" him and take him to a local jail for the night. His favorite jail was in St. Johnsbury, Vermont, where all the staff members knew him.

Eventually, this charade was discarded and they would just take him in for the night "off the books."

Given his lifestyle, it is amazing that he lived to be eighty-four. He died at St. Joseph's in Burlington, Vermont, surrounded by friends. He had lived an unusual life, especially considering his proud heritage. He is remembered as a peaceful man, watching the birds on a bench, smoking his pipe, living his life as he saw fit. An uncommon man, indeed.

Great-Grandmother Mack

Great-Grandmother Brown

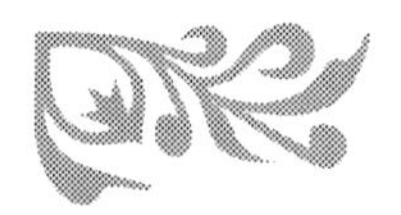 

Bagels With Wings

It was early in our marriage. Neil was at work at Fulton Fish Market, Mike was in his high chair, Will was in utero, and my in-laws were at the dining room table waiting to be served breakfast. I was feeling a tad overwhelmed and even a bit cranky. As I labored in the kitchen, I overheard my father-in-law say to my mother-in-law, "Look at the bagel she gave me. It's hard as a rock."

Something let loose inside me. "Bagels," I shouted. "You want bagels? Here." And with that I threw the rest of the bagels in his direction, cleverly missing him. I retreated to a bedroom upstairs to calm myself down and reflect on my action. What had I done? Shortly afterward, my father-in-law approached me from behind with a big bear hug. "I have no idea what I did wrong," he said earnestly, "but I'm very, very sorry."

He told this story often over the next 28 years. The gist of it was always that I threw the bagels at *him,* and *he* was the one who apologized. But his subtext was always, that girl has spunk. Mine was always, that man is smart and knows how to defuse volatile situations with hugs and humor.

We formed a close bond that day which lasted until his death in 1998 at the age of eighty-seven. How I miss that man.

My father-in-law and me, 1985

"Wait 'Til Your Father Gets Home"

My father was a kind, patient and gentle man. Like his father before him, he made his living as an engineer. But his real passion was growing things. He took great pride in his garden out back. We had fresh vegetables on the dinner table all summer long, right off the vine. His "green thumb" extending to flowering plants as well, with roses becoming a specialty of his. During the winter he would grow miniature roses inside our house under special lights. He entered his roses in local garden club contests and would invariably win first prize in most of the categories. I remember attending one of these shows and hearing someone mutter, "Who the heck is this Frank Mack?" He retired from competition soon after and became a judge.

When I think of my dad, he always has a big grin on his face and a twinkle in his eyes. He greatly enjoyed our family reunions, watching the commotion of the different generations. As adults, he called Marci and me "Kate" and "Allie," after the television show by that name (I was Kate, Marci was Allie). During our childhood, Dad would make breakfast for us kids on weekend mornings. Pancakes were his specialty, always served with real Vermont maple syrup. He was a Vermonter through and through. Born in Vermont, a graduate of the University of Vermont, and a summer resident at the Mack family cottage on Caspian Lake, near Hardwick, Vermont.

I can't remember ever seeing him angry or hearing him raise his voice, certainly not with me. I was a pretty obedient child, but got in trouble as a teenager when, as a new driver, I forgot to check the gas gauge and ran out of gas. I don't remember how I got out of this "fix" but my mother was furious with me for my carelessness. "Wait 'til your father gets home," she told me ominously. When he arrived, he asked me in a stern voice, "Paula Mack, did you run out of gas?" "Yes, Daddy," I replied. "Don't do it again." "Okay." End of discussion.

His last years on earth were not kind, as the grin and twinkle we had taken for granted were slowly extinguished by Alzheimer's disease. But they live on in our memories of him and in the family photos of our reunions taken in happier times.

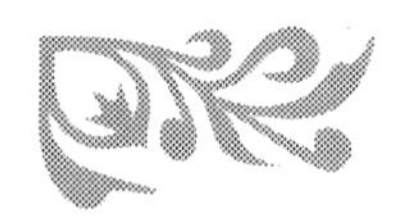

The Magic of the Written Word

What is more magical than the written word? Words on pages, black on white, sending your imagination soaring, taking you to places you never knew existed. Just twenty-six letters of the alphabet. Arranged in different combinations, they can make you laugh, or weep, or see the world through different eyes. It is magic, plain and simple.

Before I could read, I had the luxury of being read to, and that was the start of my love affair with the written word. One of my earliest memories is of sitting on Grandmother Mack's lap in Dover, Delaware as she read to me. She often described herself as a "dramatic reader" in family histories, and as a graduate of the Leland Powers School of the Spoken Word in Boston, Mass., she certainly qualified for that title. *Beauty and the Beast* was a favorite story of mine and when we would get to the end, the part about living happily ever after, I would cry, "Again!" and it would be back to page one. Chores could wait. She had a story to read to her granddaughter.

Once I could read for myself, her holiday gifts to me were always carefully chosen books, books I would cherish and read over and over again. I became the child who always had her nose in a book. The one who stayed up until three in the morning with a flashlight under the covers, unable to sleep until she found out how the story ended.

When my children were very young, I began to read to them. "Again!" Michael would cry after we finished a favorite story. One day I noticed he was reading along with me to *Seals on Wheels.* I told Neil about it that night and he dismissed it as memorization. After all, Michael was only four. He couldn't be reading.

Shortly after, we were riding along Old Country Road in Westbury when a voice from the back seat piped up, "No stopping at any time." I turned around and saw him pointing to a sign along the road. "No stopping at any time," it read. The kid could read! Soon he was reading everything. Not just books but newspaper headlines, cereal boxes, anything with words. The other mothers wanted to know my "secret." Nothing, I told them, I just read to him. Eventually, the other kids caught up and learned to read, too. But for two years, I was the mother of the little boy who could read, the child who had discovered for himself the magic of the written word.

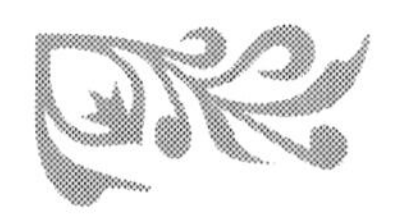

Six Kings Highway

Dover, Delaware is renowned nowadays for its Air Force Base. It is the place where the bodies of fallen service men and women are brought back to this country from overseas. But when we were growing up, we kids thought of Dover as our second home, the locale of our grandparents' house, which we visited frequently.

In retrospect, their house at Six Kings Highway was really a mansion, with five bedrooms and more rooms than we could count. There was a central spiral staircase with a wooden banister, which we would gleefully slide down. I loved looking down from the third floor bedrooms to the foyer far below. On the landings between the floors there were window seats with bookcases on both sides, and a view of the formal gardens out back. There was also an exotic forest of bamboo trees adjacent to the barn. All the houses in the neighborhood dated back to the 1800s (theirs was built in 1895). The sidewalks were made of old brick, lending to the air of antiquity. The house's central location in Dover allowed us to walk everywhere, including the public library, a movie theater, and the many stores downtown. Years later, the "haunted house" around the corner was purchased by the state, renovated, and transformed into a new governor's mansion.

Like many old houses, Six Kings Highway had its eccentricities. The entrance to the basement was through the half-bath on the first floor. There were numerous nooks and crannies on every floor for hiding spots. A large barn stood out back. We once discovered a batch of old love letters there, written by my grandfather when his engineering exploits took him far away from home. We were stunned by his expressions of deep love for my grandmother, since he was a very reserved and dignified man. There was also a large open meadow behind the barn, an ideal field for playing and exploring, Delaware's imposing government buildings looming in the background.

During World War II, my grandparents' oldest child, my Aunt Lois, moved back home with her three young children. For two years, there were four generations living under one roof, ranging in age from one to eighty, as my grandmother's mother was also living there at the time. My grandmother remembered this as a very happy period, despite worrying about the fate of my father, an Army captain, and Lois's husband, a Navy doctor stationed in the Pacific area. Luckily, both returned home unharmed, my father accompanied by his new wife, my mother, whom he had met while on duty in the mid-West.

My grandmother had been an only child and once confessed to me that she felt she had been born into the wrong family because her parents were so cold and undemonstrative. She was anything but, full of warmth and love whenever we visited. She was always happiest surrounded by young people, and after my grandfather died at home in 1966, she took in students from a nearby college and enjoyed cooking breakfast for her "boarders." She remained at Six Kings Highway until the final five years of her long life. She was eighty-five when the house was sold and she became a "guest" at a nursing home nearby. She and I kept up a regular correspondence through the years. She would complain about living among all "these old people," and I would share all the latest news about her two great-grandsons. I saved every one of her letters with their distinctive spidery handwriting. They were filled with wise advice and encouragement, and I would reread them through the years. They were among the many treasures that we lost in the 2009 fire that destroyed our home on Long Island.

When she died at age ninety in 1973, her memorial service was held at the Wesley United Methodist Church in Dover, where my grandparents had been active members since 1917. The pews were packed with her contemporaries, neighbors and many of the students who had lived with her in the late sixties. The highlight was a beautiful solo "Going Home" which left us all in tears. It's been more than forty years now but it seems like just yesterday.

My grandmother reading to my father and his sister, Lois, in 1917

Granddaddy's Bridge

As we traveled along the New Jersey Turnpike on our way to Dover, the excitement would build as we kids vied to be the first one to spot the Delaware Memorial Bridge, known to us as "Granddaddy's Bridge." Our grandfather was the Chief Engineer of Delaware from 1929 to 1950, so along with his other many accomplishments, he designed that mammoth project and oversaw every stage of its construction. With the self-centeredness of the child I was, I assumed he had it built strictly to accommodate us and make the trek shorter by eliminating the ferry portion of the trip between our house and his.

The bridge opened to traffic in 1951, the year after my grandfather took mandatory retirement at age seventy. A second span was added in 1969, making it the world's second largest twin suspension bridge. Drawings and photos of the bridge were prominently displayed at Six Kings Highway, which seemed normal to us. Since he retired when I was four, I got to spend a lot of time with my grandfather. He was a rather stern, dignified gentleman who tolerated no hi-jinks from us, but he had a soft side, too. I remember climbing onto his lap and gently rubbing his right thumb, which had been severed at the first knuckle in a sledding accident when he was young. I found this endlessly fascinating, as well as a cautionary tale about the dangers of an activity so seemingly benign as sledding.

My grandparents were both born and raised in New England, he in Vermont, she in New Hampshire. They married in 1910 and moved to Delaware in 1917. They were well known around Dover, and as their grandchildren, we were minor celebrities. We had formal portraits taken in front of their fireplace on a regular basis. Although my grandfather was one of four children, he was the only one to sire children and we were the only grandchildren to carry the Mack name. Ancestry was very important to my grandparents, as our forbears went back to the Mayflower. My grandmother was a member of the D.A.R., a regent no less, but resigned during the 1950s for reasons of conscience.

During his tenure as Chief Engineer, my grandfather supervised the dualization of US 13, the widening of the Philadelphia Pike, and was responsible for advancing tourism in Delaware by providing access to the state's beaches. He was hailed as a pioneer and innovator. But his greatest achievement was solving the complex problem of the Delaware River Crossing. A tunnel was under consideration before the final decision to build a suspension bridge was made. Both my father and my two brothers followed in his footsteps to become engineers, so I guess engineering runs in the Mack blood.

After his retirement in 1950, my grandfather remained active in civic affairs, waging letter-to-the-editor campaigns in 1959 and 1960, which led to an investigation of the State Highway Department contracts. As a result of this, the Highway Department was reorganized. This tradition of seeking out corruption was his legacy to me when I entered the newspaper business, and later as I became active in condominium affairs. It is impossible to overstate the influence that both of my grandparents had our lives.

At least twice each year, Neil and I travel over the bridge my grandfather designed. I still get a charge and a feeling of pride as we approach it. Every time. His lasting legacy: Granddaddy's Bridge.

My grandparents, Christabel and Warren Williams Mack

In the Middle

Large families were common during the 1940s and 1950s and ours was no exception. I was the second child and second daughter, followed by my brother Warren, and three years later, the baby, Christopher. In retrospect, I'm sure Marci resented giving up my parents' full attention when I arrived, just as I'm sure the arrival of the first son made me feel displaced and maybe even a bit devalued. I have no clear memories of feeling resentful during my childhood, but I do as an adult.

The setting was my parents' home in Connecticut. The occasion was a family reunion with our spouses and young children. Warren arrived after the rest of us, and my mom's face literally lit up with pleasure as she exclaimed, "Warren's here. Let the party begin!" I had to leave the room as resentment flooded my body, leaving me practically gasping in its wake. I stared at myself in the bathroom mirror, trying to calm myself down and figure out where all this emotion had come from. It's now thirty years later and I still can't get a handle on it. But don't let anyone tell you that sibling rivalry isn't real. It is.

Big families are far less common now, except in certain religious cultures, and the average American family today produces slightly less than two children. I think this is a good thing as we bid farewell to the "middle child syndrome." People may scoff, but this syndrome is very real. Just ask any middle child. It is so easy to get lost in the shuffle. You're not the first at anything and you're not the last to leave the nest. You're the monkey in the middle, vying for attention at any cost. Some of my best friends are middle kids like me. Take Sande, my old friend from Glen Rock, now living in Greenwich Village. We formed a strong bond back in the late 1950s and early 1960s when I was the family baby-sitter and her mom was like a second mother to me. Sande is my sounding board, my "go to" person for advice on any subject. My best friend Kathy was another middle child, preceded by her sister, Darien, the family star, and followed by the only son, David. During high school Kathy and I were always there for each other, cheering one another on from the sidelines. I think middle children subconsciously seek one another out, helping to make up for the deficits they experienced in their respective childhoods.

I had a brief pregnancy scare in late 1970. I was traumatized, not for myself, but at the thought that I would be making Will a middle child at a very early age. Luckily, I was just late and no measures were required to remedy the situation. After careful deliberation, I had a tubal ligation while in my late twenties, ensuring that our family size would remain at four. We have an oldest and a youngest child. None in the middle. No middle child for this child in the middle.

Our First-Born

He arrived on the first day of spring, after the long, hard winter when I lost my best friend. I remember trying to swallow my grief at her loss, terrified that it would somehow harm this much wanted child. After a brief scare in the delivery room, Michael burst onto the scene, and for me it was love at first sight.

He was a happy, easy-going baby. I took an embarrassingly huge amount of pictures of him and in each one his smile is wide, his eyes sparkling. "Michael was the first baby I ever loved," a cousin told me at a recent family wedding. It was no coincidence that she got pregnant soon after. Michael was an early talker, but before he could talk, he communicated with funny faces and clever gestures. Our townhouse in Jackson Heights was filled with the gleeful sounds of a happy child. He had a mischievous side, too. When our friends Mai Mai and Ron babysat for him while we attended a nostalgic Spring Weekend in Washington, he whimpered each time they put him in the crib. They spent the entire eight hours of our absence taking turns pacing the floor with him and patting his little back. As a consequence, it would be more than thirteen years before they finally got up the courage to have a child of their own, their beloved daughter, Hana.

When I became unexpectedly pregnant a second time in the summer of 1969, I began an indoctrination program early. I bought lots of children's books about babies and read them often to Michael. By the time Will arrived the following May, Michael greeted him eagerly. Will made the transition easy for us all by being an excellent sleeper, which allowed me to spend plenty of "alone time" with Michael. He did climb into the baby carriage once with one of Will's bottles, laughing at his own silliness.

The only difficult time was the day Michael got his first corrective leg braces at the age of two. I was in the kitchen preparing dinner when I heard the sound of glass breaking. I looked into the adjoining dining room and there was Michael, methodically breaking the wine glasses in the cabinet, one by one, in an attempt to express his rage at the unfairness of this new and unwelcome situation. I comforted him and swept up the broken shards between my tears. When we went to a cerebral palsy center for the first time soon after, he broke into a wide grin at the sight of other little boys and girls wearing leg braces, too. The child with the dancing eyes was back!

We moved soon after to Westbury, Long Island, and Michael made friends easily in the new neighborhood. His enthusiasm for life was infectious and there were few quarrels as he was always generous in sharing his toys. When his aunt and uncle sent him a magic kit for his fourth birthday, he immediately dubbed himself "Michael the Great" and began putting on magic shows for anyone within earshot. We moved to Upper Brookville in January of 1977, when he was in second grade and Will was in kindergarten. He made the transition smoothly, quickly adapting to the new, much smaller Brookville School. Music lessons were part of the after-school curriculum and he became proficient at playing the viola. Rushing to see him play in a school concert after a doctor's appointment that ran long, I entered just as it was Michael's turn. He flashed me a wide grin, then played his little heart out. The applause was deafening, but no one clapped louder than his proud mother.

Like his paternal grandfather, Michael had a talent for using his wicked sense of humor at key moments. Eventually and inevitably, sibling rivalry reared its head and Michael "ran away" from home, leaving behind a priceless note. Unfortunately, the note was lost when the house burned down, but we read and reread it so many times over the years that I have committed parts of it to memory. It began "Not So Dear Mom and Dad" and accused us of loving Will more than him. He itemized the belongings he was taking with him and signed it "Your Not So Loving Son Mike." After a brief panic, we found him in the woods behind our home. After many hugs and reassurances, all was well again in the Smith household.

A second incidence occurred shortly after Mike got his driver's license. (Somewhere along the way, he had changed his name to Mike.) Neil and I went to LaGuardia Airport to pick my mom up for a visit. We thought it was odd when we returned and my car was missing from the garage. There was a note scotch-taped on the door to the house. "Do not enter unless you promise to let me live," it began ominously. It continued: "The car is at Ray's Towing. It was the other guy's fault." Oy! We entered the house and got the complete story. In our absence, the boys decided to go for a drive along Northern Boulevard. In the vicinity of C.W. Post University, the car in front of them braked suddenly for a yellow light. Suffice it to say, Mike did not. Thankfully, no one was injured in the fender-bender, but my Oldsmobile was badly damaged. The presence of my mother and the humor of the note defused the situation. Mike is definitely Bill Smith's grandson!

Several years later, Mike headed south to the University of Miami. It was his first experience away from home and he called us every day. He was miserable. Neil and I wavered about what we should do. Then we saw the movie *Dead Poets Society.* We walked out of the theater and looked at each other and said almost simultaneously, "Mike should come home." He came back to Long Island and worked with Neil until his disability made talking on the phone and other tasks too difficult.

Mike almost died eight years ago after contracting a severe lung infection that required several surgeries. He spent a month in Aventura Hospital's intensive care unit in a coma-like state. I don't remember who suggested it, but we had his favorite music playing round the clock. The sounds of rock and roll classics drew the doctors and nurses to his room, particularly during the long, quiet evenings. Mike gradually came to and began to breathe on his own. He raised his arms in triumph. Mike was back! It took several tries, but eventually the feeding tube was disconnected. He was able to return home but has needed special care ever since. Finding the right caretaker for him was an arduous process, but eventually a miracle named Heather came into our lives and has remained with us ever since.

Mike is 44 now and the list of things he can do is much shorter than the list of things he can't. But his sense of humor is still here and his eyes still sparkle when the occasion warrants it. He is and always will be our first-born, much loved son. Our Michael.

My favorite photo of Mike (note the Kennedy button)

Love Child

He was conceived in the Summer of Love, during the August when Woodstock became a household name. Truth be told, he was not a planned child. Michael was still a toddler in diapers, just a year-and-a-half old when I first noticed the unmistakable signs of early pregnancy. A tenderness in my breasts, a feeling of nausea both day and night. Whoever named it morning sickness had obviously never been pregnant.

I remember feeling overwhelmed by this unexpected turn of events, but excited, too, about the new life stirring within me. A playmate for Michael, possibly the little girl I had always longed for. By the time of Will's birth the following May, Michael was out of diapers and eager to meet his new sibling. The birth went relatively smoothly and Neil was able to accompany me into the delivery room this time. He remembers my look of utter shock when they told me we had another son. I was so certain this child would be a girl that we hadn't even discussed boys' names ahead of time.

He was close to nine pounds at birth, the biggest baby in the nursery, so the staff used him to demonstrate child-care techniques to the other mothers at New York Hospital. He was perfect, not a mark on him, looking more like a month-old baby than a scrawny newborn. After a brief scare when he developed jaundice, during which I overheard one doctor joke about the carefully laid-out pale yellow "going home" outfit matching the baby's skin color, we headed home to Jackson Heights to introduce Michael to his still unnamed sibling. Will's birth certificate stated "Baby Boy Smith" until we settled on the name Willis a few weeks later. That choice was inspired by Willis Reed, who had led the New York Knicks to a basketball championship the night before I gave birth. The name was obviously Neil's idea. I did have some input though, vetoing the alternate choice, Walter, after Walt Frazier, as sounding too old-fashioned.

We held a bris for Will when he was eight days old and passed him around on a pillow like a little prince for all to admire. He slept through it all, except for the actual circumcision, during which he and I both cried like babies. In fact, Will was an unusually easy baby, a good sleeper and voracious eater who rarely fussed. Mike would sit in my lap as I rocked and nursed the newest member of the clan, talking or listening to stories as I read and Mike turned the pages. He became my little helper, bringing diapers or whatever else I needed. My sisters-in-law were horrified that I had again declined to hire a baby nurse. I opted instead for extra help with housekeeping, a task I felt was far less important than taking care of my little ones.

Having been a second child myself, I was always very careful not to let Will feel less important than his older brother. I planned a family party for his first birthday, ordering a special cake in the shape of a toy block from Ebinger's bakery, which was *the* bakery in Queens in those days. It escaped my notice in planning this celebration that May 9th that year was Mother's Day. One by one, people called to cancel until we were down to just the four of us. I wept at the perceived slight, but in all the photos, Will is beaming as he attacks the giant cake with gusto, a fork in each hand. We invited in the neighborhood children to share the goodies. In years to come I made sure not to schedule his birthday party on Mother's Day.

The boys' closeness in age was really a blessing, as they became playmates and good friends, particularly once Will began walking and talking. How fascinating though that they were so different from one another right from birth. Michael resembled the Smith side of the family; Will looked like a Mack. Michael excelled in verbal skills and reading; Will was far more interested in how things worked. He spent hours taking things apart and putting them back together, sometimes correctly, sometimes "creatively." To this day, Will is greatly skilled at computer imaging and all kinds of photography, as well as ably serving as a disc jockey at parties. He was also far more daring than Michael, which resulted in numerous frantic trips to local emergency rooms.

While Neil and I were away in New York in the summer of 1996, Will proposed to his girlfriend, Brenda. We had great fun planning the wedding for the Memorial Day weekend of 1997, which turned into a family reunion for the Mack side of the family. Thirteen months later, Will and Brenda presented us with the greatest gift of all, our grandson Jordan. I was beside myself with joy. I remember someone in the condo asking if I was disappointed that he wasn't a girl, answering huffily that I couldn't possibly love him any more. I probably got a bit carried away in my enthusiasm for being a grandmother as my hand-written card from Will on Mother's Day read: "To a great mom and an even better grandma."

I treasure that card just as I treasure the author, Will, our second born, much-loved baby boy. He is 42 now but he'll always be my baby.

Will at his graduation from Locust Valley High in 1988

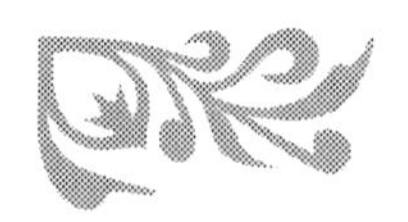 

Oh, What a Grandchild!

We have just one grandchild. Many of our friends have four or more, but Neil and I have only one, our Jordan. And yet, we consider ourselves to be fortunate because some of our friends have no grandchildren and no prospects of ever having a grandchild. I can't even imagine this, because it is grandchildren that keep us young (while, of course, wearing us out). It is grandchildren that keep the family lineage going into the future. They *are* our future.

Also, this is not just any grandchild. I know, I know, every grandparent thinks theirs is special, but in the case of our Jordan, it's true. He was an incredible baby, adorable, smart and funny, a lot like his proud daddy. When the class photos were distributed at his Montessori school, I always felt sorry for the other parents and grandparents, because their kids were so plain and ours was so good looking! The dimples, the light sprinkling of freckles across his nose and cheeks, the almond-shaped eyes.

Today Jordan is a strapping young man at that awkward age of fourteen. He is still adorable, but in a more manly way now. He's still funny by nature. I have new stories to tell my friends after almost every visit. Still smart. Sometimes I wonder where he gets his wizardly abilities with all things electronic and then I remember that I am descended from a long line of engineers on the Mack side of the family. And so is Jordan.

Back in 1990, we watched a home video at Ron and Mai Mai's house in Chapel Hill, North Carolina. The occasion was Ron's parents' fiftieth wedding anniversary. Ron's mother, "Mrs. G," had the microphone and said these words. "People say to me, 'You have only one grandchild.' And I reply, 'But oh, what a grandchild!' "

I've never forgotten those words. They were pure poetry, spoken with such love and pride about her "only" grandchild, Hana. I remember thinking how lucky Hana was to be so beloved. And how lucky Mr. and Mrs. G. were to have such a talented and beautiful granddaughter. A win-win situation for all concerned.

Little did I know that eight years later, Neil and I would be joining that exclusive club, the one restricted to doting grandparents every where. We have just one grandchild, Jordan Taylor Smith. But oh, what a grandchild!

"Don't Sweat the Small Stuff"

My mom used a phrase often during her final decades. "Don't sweat the small stuff," she'd say when I complained about traffic or a balky appliance or any of life's minor annoyances. It was good advice and I repeated it to myself often, particularly when I was having a bad day. It is only now looking back at her life that I can see this was a lesson she had taught herself only after spending many long years worrying about what other people thought.

My mom was a child of the Depression and it affected her life in many ways. She was the youngest of seven children born to her parents, who immigrated to Illinois from Kovno, Lithuania, around 1900. Her father died in an industrial accident when she was only four, so she had few memories of him. Her mother became the family breadwinner, with the children helping out whenever possible. Fortunately, her father had acquired a number of properties and the income from these helped pay the bills. But as the Depression deepened, renters could not afford to pay their bills and the family relied on income from a movie theater it owned. At the age of eleven, my mother was in charge of the concession stand. She not only waited on the customers, she kept track of the inventory, too. This was in addition to attending public school, where she managed to skip a grade and win academic awards. Even though she was well qualified, college was out of the question due to financial concerns, and she went right to work after high school.

Her lack of a college degree must have bothered her no end, especially when she married my father, who came from a family of means where all the children went to boarding schools and then universities. We four children always knew that we would be going to college after high school. The choice of schools was up to us, but not going was never an option. We all left home after high school: Marci to Lycoming College, me to American University, Warren to Bucknell University and later, Harvard Business School, and Chris to the University of Arizona.

I remember having arguments with my mother on only a few occasions. The first was when I announced in the summer of 1966 that I was marrying Neil and converting to Judaism. I don't know what reaction I expected to this news but it wasn't the one I got. Her first response was, "I thought you were going to marry a senator." (I am embarrassed to admit that it was indeed my stated goal when I left home for Washington, D.C. in the fall of 1964. This was before women's liberation opened up a world of choices.) Her second response was that there would be no wedding announcement in the local newspaper. The conversation went downhill from there and I ended up accusing her of being prejudiced and she slapped me for the first and only time in my life. I left the house in a huff and called Neil, who came to my rescue. Looking back, I think the conversion announcement was particularly painful for her to hear, especially given her own conversion from Catholicism to Protestantism and the enormous guilt she carried within her about that decision. But she was also very upset that, unlike my sister, I was marrying before getting my college degree. Neil and I were doing so for the most conventional of reasons. We wanted to be together as much as possible and living together without marriage simply wasn't an option in those days.

My dad patched things up by taking me aside and explaining that my mother was going through a tough time emotionally and they would support our marriage in whatever way was needed. Both my parents walked me down the aisle of the Glen Rock Jewish Center the following January, my dad with a wide grin, my mom looking like she was praying for the earth to open up and swallow her whole. I was oblivious to this at the time but it is very apparent in the wedding photographs. An announcement of our marriage appeared in the local papers, including the location of the wedding. Which no doubt caused tongues to wag in the community, which I was also oblivious to.

In the summer of 1967, Neil and I moved to New York and I enrolled in Queens College for my senior year. I became pregnant with Michael, which was a huge relief to Neil's parents, who feared he would be drafted and sent to Viet Nam. In 1967, there was still a deferment for fathers, though it was terminated shortly afterward. As a lover of babies, I was thrilled to be pregnant, but telling my mother weighed heavily on me. I waited until the end of a long phone call, then blurted out the news. There was a long pause. A very long pause. Finally, she asked, "What about finishing college?" I told her I'd do my best to finish before the baby came, though in actuality, it would be ten years before I finally earned my degree. I could feel her sharp disapproval right through the telephone wires.

My mother eventually adjusted to the new reality and delighted in the birth of her first grandchild, just as later she would learn to adjust when my sister Marci divorced, followed by both my brothers. Along the way, she learned to stop caring about what other people thought and just go with the flow. She became a much happier person as a result and left behind that child of the Depression and the guilt she felt so deeply when she married out of her faith. She learned to stop sweating the small stuff and embrace the good things life had to offer. She left that legacy to her children and grandchildren. And we are all the better for it.

My mother in 1939

Where's the Bottle?

Breast-feeding is pretty widespread these days, but it wasn't in 1968 when our first child was born. I studied motherhood before Michael's arrival and everything I read said that "the breast is best," so I never considered not breast-feeding.

What no one told me was that, while a natural act, breast-feeding isn't so easy, especially in the beginning. Michael was born in New York Hospital's Lying-In section, which meant that four new mothers shared a spacious room and attached nursery with their four infants. This was an ideal set-up for spending a lot of time with your newborn and for nursing on demand. The babies could be with you all day and then the nurses put them back in the nursery at night. The first two days were easy because my milk had not yet come in and the baby was satisfied with the colostrum provided. I asked the nurses to wake me up on the second night but they ignored my instructions and gave him a bottle in the middle of the night. Morning came and my breasts were engorged with milk and I held a baby in my arms who wasn't particularly hungry. I was in tears when Neil showed up. He pulled the curtain around us for privacy and helped me calm down and get Michael to learn how to "latch on." What a relief, both for my sore breasts and my fervent desire to give Michael a head start by nursing him. These days they have "lactation nurses" to help new mothers. (If he ever quits the seafood business, this could be a new career path for Neil.)

Nursing Michael was easy going after that. My only problem was that in the early months, I had a little trouble with the "let down" reflex. On a trip to Yonkers Raceway to watch our horse, Parader Lobell, in competition, Neil and I were in the paddock area when someone asked about our new baby, whom we had left at home with my parents. Instantly, two big milk stains appeared on the front of my light gray jacket. I spent the entire evening clutching the racing program tightly to my bosom to hide the dark stains. Thankfully, within a few weeks I got this trigger mechanism under control.

We didn't go out much during the early days of parenthood, so one particular occasion stands out. We were attending a Passover dinner in Neil's brother's house in East Hills. It was a rather formal affair around a large, beautifully set dining room table. I cradled Michael in my left arm as I ate with the other. At one point, Michael became fussy and my sister-in-law led me to a comfortable chair in the master bedroom where I could nurse Michael in private. My nephew David, then three, wandered in and asked, "What are you doing, Aunt Paula?" "Feeding Michael," was the reply. With a look of puzzlement he asked, "Where's the bottle?" I patiently explained that some babies are fed with bottles and others drink their mother's milk. He nodded his head slowly then went into the dining room to declare, "You won't believe what Aunt Paula is doing in the bedroom!" Nervous laughter all around. What would that "hippie" Neil married think of next?

Charity Clapp

When studying genealogy, you just never know what you'll find.

My mom's parents immigrated to America from Kovno, Russia (later Lithuania) around 1900 and became American citizens in 1919, the same year my mother was born. Her parents cut off all ties with relatives left behind when they came here, in part to protect them from any retaliation, and partly to start their new life afresh. My sister Marci and I were both named for my mother's parents, Paul and Marcella Zeimis. My grandfather Paul, for whom I was named, died when my mom was just four in an accident. We met our grandmother, Marcella, only a few times through the years, as my mom's entire family lived in the Illinois area, many long miles from our home in New Jersey.

I never knew where Neil's grandparents came from until we helped our grandson Jordan with a school project involving family trees. Aunt Edna, the youngest of my father-in-law's many siblings, was called upon for information and I was dumbfounded to hear her inform me of her parents' hometown. "Kovno," she told me. "It's now part of Lithuania." Neil and I were taken aback by the coincidence. Had our respective grandparents known each other in the "old country?" It was certainly possible. Could one or both of my grandparents have been Jewish and converted to Catholicism when they came to America? That was another intriguing possibility.

Tracing my father's roots was a much easier task. Long before it became a popular pastime, my grandfather and his father before him spent many long hours researching the family's ancestry. My maiden name, Mack, has a long history in this country. The first of the line, John Mack, immigrated to Massachusetts in 1669 from Inverness, Scotland. (It was conjectured that Mack was a shortened version of McDougall or McGregor or another Scottish clan name that was changed by the king in retaliation for insubordination.) Six of John Mack's grandchildren fought in the Revolutionary War. His great-granddaughter, Lucy Mack Smith, was the mother of Joseph Smith, Jr., the founder of the Mormon Church. Lucy's grandfather, Ebenezer Mack, was the brother of Nehemiah Mack, my great-great-great-great-grandfather.

Elisha Mack, one of Nehemiah's eight children, married Jane White in 1803. She was a lineal descendant of William White of the Mayflower colony. She was also descended from William Bradford, the first governor of Plymouth Colony. She was the daughter of Resolved White and Charity Clapp. I know nothing further about Charity Clapp, other than the fact that she was my great-grandfather's great-grandmother. But you have to love such a colorful name. Jane White Mack's son, Resolved Mack, married Mary Bancroft in 1838 and it is her portrait that hangs above our fireplace today in our home in New York. I find this portrait, which was painted around the time of the Civil War, endlessly fascinating. Her gaze is unflinching, her hair pulled tightly back from her face but adorned with a lacy headband. Not even a trace of a smile about her pursed lips. How amazing that this portrait still exists more than 150 years after it was painted, and how fortunate that it was in our Florida condo when our house burned down in 2009.

Much of the information above concerning the Mack family history is derived from a paper published by my great-grandfather, Henry Resolved Mack, in 1914. In the preface, he intones rather solemnly, "It is a good thing to have ancestors to one's credit, but better to be a credit to one's ancestors." Almost 100 years later, that premise still holds. Plus, it would make an excellent fortune cookie saying.

FRIENDS

Friends and their importance in our lives cannot be overstated. Growing up I had a series of "best friends." The last one was Kathy, who played a major supporting role during my tumultuous high school years. I was so traumatized by her suicide in 1967 that I could not even mention her name or write about her for decades. When I finally did, it was an essay published in the New York Times *in 1987, titled "Best Friends: Love and Loss Forever." The last line read, "I've had many friends since Kathy died but I'll never have another best friend."*

I have been so lucky since Kathy's death to have lived a life that has been greatly enriched by many close friendships. There is an expression, the bond of friendship, which perfectly expresses what my friends mean to me. We are bonded together by shared experiences and viewpoints and histories. We sometimes talk in shorthand just like old married couples. It is impossible for me to imagine a life without my good friends. But I still avoid using that "best friend" designation. Partly out of loyalty to Kathy and partly out of the fear, irrational though it may be, that putting that designation on another person might somehow bring them bad luck. So I use other terms to describe my good friends. Close. Beloved. Dear. Cherished. Anything but "best."

The Nudge

Behind every person who accomplishes something in life, there is someone else, pushing him forward, urging her on. Telling him he can do it. Sometimes it is a parent, sometimes it is a spouse, and sometimes it is a mentor or good friend. I call this person the "nudge."

My nudge is my dear friend Elaine Frisher. I have known Elaine for years, as a neighbor in my Florida condo, a fellow mah jongg player, and a friend who is always there for me. Our friendship began over a shared admiration for Serena Williams, the tennis player, who is a neighbor and close friend of Elaine's granddaughter. Like everyone else in Elaine's family, Serena calls Elaine "Momma."

Although twenty years separate Elaine and me, she feels more like a contemporary. She has such an enthusiasm for life, especially for the members of her large extended family. She greets her many friends with such warmth that she makes them feel valued and cherished.

For years, Elaine has been urging me to get back to writing. She finally wore me down, and now, thanks to my favorite "nudge," I am writing again and I have never been happier or felt more fulfilled. Words cannot express how grateful I am to Elaine for her friendship and support.

"Five Again"

One summer seven years ago, four friends from Long Island and I got together to form our own "Joy Luck Club." Our friend Lois had been playing mah jongg for decades, so she served as our tutor, our "maven." With good humor and infinite patience, she taught us novices the intricacies of this complicated game. To say that we were slow learners would be a vast understatement.

Elaine assumed the thankless role of organizer, no easy task with our busy schedules. It's Elaine who makes the phone calls and, more often than not, serves as hostess and chief baker. From scratch no less. She is the "heart" of our group.

Val is our "class act," never leaving her house until her hair and makeup are perfect, her outfit accessorized just so. She has an air of quiet dignity and calm about her that the rest of us can only envy. When we play at Val's, the spread is abundant, the table settings up to Martha Stewart's high standards.

Joan is the baby of the group. She's the only one still working full time, so we need to fit our games around her ever-changing schedule. When we play at Joan's, concentrating is a real challenge. It is always a chaotic scene, with the phones and doorbell ringing constantly, the grand babies interrupting, the dog and husband making their appearances. She juggles it all effortlessly, never losing her cool or focus, her sense of humor intact. She is our "wonder woman."

I am the fifth member, the "fair weather friend." Each year, I leave Long Island for Florida in late September and return in early June. I miss my "girls" all winter long but we stay in touch. Through the years, we've celebrated successes together, including Elaine's mid-life bat mitzvah, and helped each other cope with misfortunes, including cancer, the loss of a spouse, and the divorces of several of our children. We are there for one another, through good times and bad. It's not just about the game.

Since four of us have summer birthdays, several times each year we "surprise" the birthday honoree with a cake and an off-key rendition of "Happy Birthday." A few years ago, Val surprised me with a different cake when I returned from Florida. On it was a simple, heart-felt message. "Five Again."

Class act, indeed.

The Best Man

When we were first married, Neil was called upon to serve as "best man" at a large number of weddings. Many of the grooms were longtime friends from Pine Lake Park, a summer bungalow community near Peekskill, New York. Ron and Howie, Mike and Art, Neil had a key role to play at all their nuptials as I sat in the audience watching the proceedings. Neil was also best man at the wedding of a college friend, Tim, from George Washington University. In the years since, the bonds of friendship eroded, some sooner than others, and we've lost track of all of the grooms with the exception of Ron, who has continued to play a major role in our lives.

There was another wedding, this one in 1982, which took place near our home on Long Island where Neil served as best man. Neil's friend Stu, a fellow harness racing owner and fan, was marrying his long-time love, Erika, known to all by her nickname Riki. The setting was the Muttontown Preserve and the weather cooperated as they took their vows on a picture perfect summer afternoon beside a lovely pond. A reception followed at the Maine Maid Inn in nearby Jericho.

Stu and Riki are still very much a part of our lives. We see them often each summer on Long Island and once each winter for a few hectic days when they come to Florida to escape the cold and visit Riki's relatives. They know us so well that on one visit, they gave us an amazing book, *Good Without God* by Greg Epstein, which makes the most convincing argument I've ever read for morality without faith, something Neil and I both believe in strongly. We've known their two kids, Jenny and Mikey, since their births and have had the great pleasure of watching them mature into bright, funny young adults whom are a joy to be around. They call us Aunt Paula and Uncle Neil, even though we aren't related by blood. But in truth, all four of them feel more like close family than friends.

When Riki and Stu held a joint party several years ago to celebrate Jenny's college graduation and Mikey's high school graduation in their Albertson backyard, we were among those invited. As we sat around, someone, possibly Riki's sister, asked how Neil came to know Stu. The party turned silent as the guests awaited an answer. I don't remember the exact reply but I know it was inadequate. It is hard to explain what motivates a friendship of many years that isn't based on ties to a shared childhood, a camp, a school, a neighborhood or a profession. Sometimes someone comes along and you realize that here is somebody you want to keep in your life just because his friendship enriches it.

That's how it is with Stu, and, of course, Riki and Jenny and Mike. There is no expiration date on our longtime friendship. Lucky us, lucky them.

The Ava Gardner of Aventura

We are born into families, but during our lifetimes, if we are very lucky, we acquire some really good friends along the way. They are there for us to celebrate life's triumphs, big and small, and help us through the rough patches. I have friends who have lived charmed lives, with a minimum of loss and grief. They are the lucky ones. Most of us aren't that lucky and have scars, external and internal, to show for it.

After 9/11, despite the horror of that day, I breathed a sigh of relief that the events hadn't directly impacted any of my close friends and neighbors. Only to find out when I returned to Florida, that one of my friends from another Mystic Pointe tower, Adele, had lost her son-in-law, Alan Feinberg. Alan was a firefighter from New Jersey, assigned to a New York City precinct, and left home on that crisp September morning never to return. He left behind his family, Adele's daughter, Wendy, and their two children, to pick up the pieces. Aiding in this were, of course, my friend Adele and her husband, Steve.

Our friendship has grown exponentially since then. She was there for me when my mom died four years ago. I was there for her when Steve got sick, then passed away. We meet every Sunday for brunch when I'm in Florida to talk about the week gone by, to share secrets and beauty tips. Let me tell you, this is one gorgeous lady! I always try to look my best on Sunday mornings but she manages to outshine me every time. Hair and makeup perfect, outfit coordinated just so. The Ava Gardner of Aventura! As beautiful inside as she is on the outside.

It's no wonder that there is a new man in her life now. She tells me that Bernie, a wonderful bear hug of a man, puts her on a pedestal. Where else would one put this vivacious, lovely and caring lady?

De-Friending Mildred

After my family, the most important people in my life are my friends. I have been blessed through the years with many close friends and I cherish them all. When Bette Midler sings "You Gotta Have Friends" on my iPod, I sing along at the top of my voice. When my friend Elly died of ovarian cancer at the age of fifty, James Taylor's "You've Got a Friend" was playing on my car radio as I pulled up to the house to pay a condolence call. It took me at least ten minutes to compose myself. Simon and Garfunkel's "Bridge Over Troubled Water" always makes me think of our beloved friends, Mai Mai and Ron, who have been there for us, through good times and bad, for almost fifty years. Through the Internet and frequent visits, I stay in touch with Sande from Glen Rock; Anna, my American University roommate; and neighbors from the various places we have lived over the years. Not to mention my mah jongg buddies in New York and Florida.

I would do anything for my friends, including giving them the shirt off my back if they needed it. But some friendships reach an expiration date. That is what happened in the spring of 2008 to my relationship with a former neighbor named "Mildred." We had met in our condo in Aventura when she was married to a retired newspaper executive. He and I bonded over our mutual love of journalism and politics. When they decided condo living was not for them, they moved to a house in a gated community in Pembroke Pines and we saw them occasionally for dinner. After Len died, I called Mildred frequently and met her occasionally for lunch to help ease her loneliness.

Then came the presidential election of 2008. I knew that Mildred was a strong supporter of Hillary Clinton. She was aware that Neil and I were equally strong supporters of Barack Obama. We met for lunch in May and midway through the meal, I opened my jacket to reveal my vibrant red t-shirt with Obama's smiling face and the slogan "Yes We Can!!!" Her reaction shocked me to the core. "Yuck," she said loudly with an expression of extreme distaste on her face. She came just short of spitting on me. Her face mirrored the expressions I had seen on white bystanders in old newsreels about the integration of the public schools in Little Rock, Arkansas. I saw hatred, based not on ideology but skin color.

The meal ended shortly after. So did the friendship. I debated just avoiding her by not returning her calls but that would have been the coward's way out. I am a lot of things but I am not a coward. I called her up and told her that her reaction had both saddened and horrified me. "We are judged by the company we keep," I told her. She tried half-heartedly to defend herself and then we said our goodbyes.

I know I did the right thing but I still feel a bit conflicted. And I can't bring myself to cross out her name and phone number from my address book. They remain there, under "M," right after a long list of Macks.

Two Survivors

I have two friends I hold dear. They don't know each other and are from two different generations, but they have a lot in common. They are both Jewish and are both survivors of childhoods marked by unimaginable horrors. Despite their pasts, both have gone on to become valuable members of society, transforming the ugliness of their childhood nightmares by confronting them head on and sharing their experiences with others. To do this requires a special kind of courage, one that the rest of us can only admire with awe. I feel so privileged to count Sue and Magda among my friends.

Sue was born in Washington, D.C. in 1946, where her father was a high official in the Truman administration. The family later moved to the West Indies, then finally settled in Glen Rock, N.J. in 1958. This is when our lives intersected. They lived in the most upscale neighborhood in town and her father drove a fancy Cadillac Fleetwood. Sue quickly became a member of the "in" crowd and a straight-A student. Her closet was filled with all the "right" clothes and shoes. I remember envying her "perfect" life. Never in a million years could I have suspected that behind those closed doors, she was being sexually molested by her own father.

She learned to survive by keeping her eyes tightly closed and pretending to be someone else. After graduating from Boston University, Sue tried repeatedly to tell her story through works of fiction. It wasn't until her parents died within six days of one another in 1992, that Sue felt free to tell her story in a factual, non-fictional way. She produced her memoir, *Because I Remember Terror, Father, I Remember You*, in just three months. It was received with great acclaim and she became a sought-after speaker on the subject of child sexual abuse. She followed it with another memoir, *Love Sick,* which was turned into a Lifetime movie, along with a book of poetry and a well-received writer's guide to memoir writing. She is currently a professor at the Vermont College of Fine Arts, where she teaches a writing program for students with advanced degrees in literature. She continues to speak out about her childhood to help others, an act requiring incredible courage.

Magda's childhood was very different. I have known Magda for many years in our Florida community, where we have played tennis together and shared many long lunches. I was aware that she was a Holocaust survivor, but only learned the details of her ordeal recently. Magda was born in 1930 in Czechoslovakia, the youngest of seven children. She remembers her parents as wonderful, kind, quiet hard-working people. When the Germans took over in 1944, Magda and her sisters were separated from their parents and an older married sister by the infamous Joseph Mengele. They never saw each other again. The three remaining sisters were taken by cattle car to Auschwitz-Birkenau, where they were ordered to disrobe, have their heads shaved and get disinfected. No shoes, no underwear, no personal belongings. So much for the jewelry their mother had carefully sewn into the lining of their coats. They never let on that they were sisters, as they feared they would be intentionally separated in a bid to cause them even more pain and suffering. At one point, Magda was separated from her sisters because she looked frailer and younger, but an exchange was arranged during the night with another separated family. This action undoubtedly saved Magda's life.

After months of enduring the black smoke and terrible smells from the nearby crematoriums, not to mention extreme hunger and cold, the sisters were relocated to northern Germany to work in an ammunition factory under the watchful eyes of the SS soldiers. They were liberated by American soldiers in April of 1945, after which they lived in England and then finally America, where Magda earned her college degree and began a rewarding teaching career spanning 26 years. She married her husband Sam in 1956, after meeting him on the tennis courts of Central Park, and they raised two daughters together. Along with her children and six grandchildren, art remains her passion as does speaking to children in the local schools about the Holocaust. Despite all she has been through, she remains optimistic about the future and is one of the kindest and most empathetic people I have ever known. I think of Magda as the embodiment of Anne Frank had she survived the Holocaust.

Two women. Two survivors. Two prime examples of people who overcame unspeakable evil to go on to triumph by living productive, meaningful lives.

Life is the catchall category of this book. It's the place for all the stories that don't fit the other designations, for musings about religion and birth signs, racism and cancer, feminism and condo living, and high school reunions and bad hair days and the never-ending search for happiness. When I e-mail close friends, "life" is often the subject line I utilize.

So many things happen to us as we go about our daily lives. Many are traumatic as we experience them, but amusing in hindsight. They make for great storytelling.

Life is at times messy and complicated and exhilarating and boring. I lost a lot of contemporaries to cancer and other diseases when we were only in our fifties. Because of this, I realize perhaps more than most what a precious gift life truly is. What a privilege it is to grow old with our spouses, see out children mature, and get to meet our grandchildren and participate in their lives. I try never to take that privilege for granted and to savor each day. Every day. Every moment.

CAROUSEL

The first ride any child gets on is a carousel. To a small child, the horse seems enormous, the ups and downs steep, the music magical, and the constant whirl dizzying. At first, a parent stands next to the child making sure he or she doesn't fall off. Eventually, the child rides alone with his parents off to the side, holding their breath as the child disappears then reappears, worrying when he lets go to wave with one hand. Eventually, the child outgrows the carousel and moves on to roller coasters and rides like Disney World's Space Mountain. But the carousel is part of almost every young child's life.

One of my all-time favorite movies is *Carousel.* It was released in 1956 when I was ten and it made a huge impression on me. Initially, I identified with Louise Bigelow, the young daughter of Billy Bigelow and Shirley Jones's character, Julie Jensen. But as I matured, I also identified with Julie. The musical, one of Rogers and Hammerstein's best, contains some of their most famous songs, including "If I Loved You" and "You'll Never Walk Alone." But the one I remember best is "What's the Use of Wondering." I guess I favor that particular song because I've always been drawn to "bad" boys, the kind that flaunt convention and color outside the lines. I spent my childhood trying extra hard to be perfect in an attempt to win my parents' attention. So naturally, I'm drawn to the opposite personality type. Anyone who knows my husband knows I followed my heart when I married this guy.

I think of life as like one big carousel. The ride starts slowly and scenes flash by as it revolves. Faces of people both familiar and unknown are part of the view. Sometimes it lurches to a halt, taking your breath away momentarily. But eventually it starts up again, with its ups and downs, ups and downs, relentlessly, until finally the ride slowly comes to a halt. It's not about the destination but the journey. My greatest fear is that someday, like my dad, I'll develop Alzheimer's and become unaware of life's carousel. The sights will remain unseen, even the memory of the ride and its ups and downs gone as if they had never happened. And all the faces, even those of the ones we love, become strangers. The saddest day of my mother's life, the one that broke her heart, was the day my father no longer recognized her.

My fervent wish for myself, and all the people I care about, is that we be present for it all, the good and the bad, the ups and the downs.

The carousel that we call life.

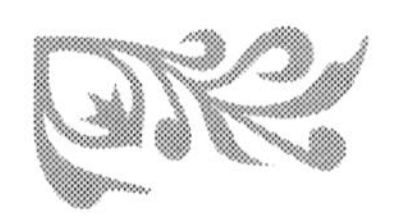 

The Pursuit of Happiness

There's a great quote early in the classic film *The Big Chill.* Chloe, the young girlfriend of the man who committed suicide, is asked by one of his college friends if she knew he was unhappy. Her reply: "I haven't met that many happy people in my life. How do they act?"

The "pursuit of happiness" is guaranteed to every American. It's in the Declaration of Independence, right after life and liberty. Such an interesting choice of words from our founding fathers. And yet happiness remains elusive for so many people. What is happiness? For one person it could be feeling safe and loved. To another, it could be an adventure into new territory. To a third, succeeding in their chosen profession. For some, it is fame. Or a warm puppy. Making slow, sensuous love. A fabulous theater experience or concert or meal. The possibilities are endless.

I'm very partial to a Will Rogers quote: "Most folks are about as happy as they make up their minds to be." In other words, the burden is on the individual to find his or her own path to a happy life. I am eliminating clinically depressed people from this discussion because I don't think choice is involved for them. I went through a short miserable period of depression seven years ago due to a rare response to a cortisone shot. I call this my period of "circling the drain." It was all I could do to survive, much less be happy or even pretend to be happy. I couldn't even enjoy eating, as food tasted like ashes. Then slowly the cloud lifted and I became myself again. My inner ballerina had returned.

I believe we have a choice in how we greet each day and respond to events that are beyond our control. There are a myriad of choices we face every day of our lives. We spend far too much time worrying about bad things that will never happen and far too little celebrating the good things that do.

The next time you find yourself feeling happy, relish it. Prolong it. You deserve it. It says so right in our Declaration of Independence.

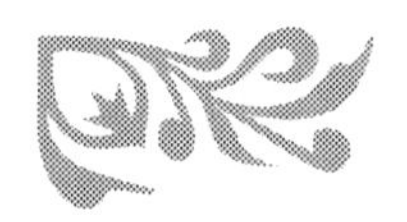

The Jewish Mermaid

I have a complicated relationship with religion. I was born a Catholic (my mother's religion), raised as a Protestant (my father's religion), and became a Jewish convert at the age of 20.

Books have always played a major role in my life, and *The Rabbi* by Noah Gordon was a bestseller in the 1960s. The story revolves around a gentile woman who falls in love with a rabbi and converts to Judaism. I thought it was one of the most romantic books I had ever read. When I fell in love with my future husband, Neil, who happened to be Jewish, I started planning my conversion shortly after our engagement in the summer of 1966. Were there other factors involved in my decision to convert? Of course. My closeness to Momma Nancy and her family was certainly one. Another was the knowledge that my mother had left the Catholic Church early in her marriage, between my birth and Warren's. (Marci and I didn't even learn that we had been baptized as Catholics until we were confirmed in a Protestant church as teenagers.) My conversion was probably also an attempt on my part to please my future in-laws, especially my mother-in-law. And finally, I felt no real connection to the church I was raised in. As teenagers, Kathy and I used to volunteer to staff the nursery school during the Sunday services. This was our way of getting out of attending church while being together and playing with the children, something we both enjoyed.

I could have opted for a Reformed conversion, but I wanted to do it the hard way. I timed it for the Wednesday before our January wedding in a conservative Glen Rock, New Jersey temple. The night before, I called my father-in-law-to-be in tears, terrified that I would be rejected, and thus unable to marry in the temple that weekend. He calmly reassured me, promising that whatever happened, we would work something out. His positive attitude was contagious, enabling me to get a much-needed good night's sleep.

I had read up on the tenets of the Jewish faith and studied diligently under the rabbi at American University in Washington, D.C., where I was in the middle of my junior year. I had already taken a non-credit course in Yiddish with him, and, truth be told, I was a bit of a teacher's pet. On conversion day, he introduced me to a formidable looking board of rabbis for what felt a bit like an inquisition. Unlike most religions, Judaism does not encourage converts. In fact, it actually discourages potential converts. (If you don't believe me, watch the episode of *Sex and the City* where Charlotte decides to become a Jew.) True to form, the board of rabbis played hard to get, but I won them over with my knowledge and earnestness.

Next came the mikvah, the ritual bath. First the female attendant prepared me, making sure there were no tangles in the hair on my head or any other part of my body, and that my fingernails were cut very short and unpolished. I then plunged into the murky water, recited the required prayers as the rabbis listened through a partially open door, and emerged a Jewish mermaid with a new name, Ruth P'nina. All female converts are given the name Ruth, which happens to be my mother's name. P'nina is the Hebrew name for pearl.

I met Neil outside afterward, triumphantly clutching my conversion papers in my hand, my long hair soaking wet in the January chill. I was a Jewess with papers to prove it! The wedding was on! I told Neil about my promises to the rabbis, that I would keep a kosher home and follow all the rules of my new faith. "Forget it," replied this former student of Yeshiva of Central Queens. End of discussion.

My conversion papers were lost forever when our Long Island home in Upper Brookville burned to the ground in 2009, and I haven't seen the inside of a temple in longer than I care to admit. But inside, I still feel Jewish to my very core. Once a Jewish mermaid, always a Jewish mermaid.

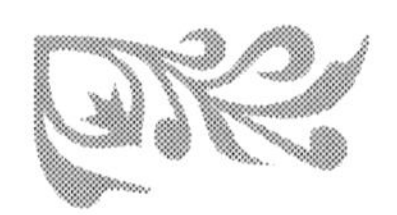

Best Foot Forward

I was a face in the crowd in my high school. Never one to stand out, my grades were good but not outstanding, and I always preferred hanging out with my best friend Kathy to being part of any particular clique. Then came my junior year and the try-outs for the class play, *Best Foot Forward*. Something happened to me when I got up on that stage. I became fearless. I was funny. I killed, as they say in the comedy world. It was a completely ad-libbed performance and I have no memory of what I actually said. No one in the auditorium that day was more surprised than me by my impromptu act. Perhaps my inner ballerina was whispering in my ear as I stood on the stage.

When the list of the "chosen" was posted, my name was up there. I had won the role of Ethel, the part played on Broadway by Liza Minnelli. I remember a popular girl turning away with tears in her eyes, bitterly disappointed that she had lost out to me, a nobody. I was giddy with triumph and took great care selecting a dress for the play. It was a knee-length, turquoise chiffon sheath with a little cape that I purchased at Mandee's, a local shop along our town's main street, Rock Road. After arduous rehearsals, we put on two performances. I thrived in the spotlight, enjoying my time on stage immensely. I didn't want it to end.

Years later, it was our grandson's turn to be in the spotlight at a production at his Montessori school. He was a reluctant participant until I told him about the thrill I got appearing on stage in high school. He became more enthusiastic as the evening of the play approached but was outraged at having to wear stage makeup. "Makeup is for girls not boys," he declared firmly. But when he appeared onstage and the spotlight shone on him, he nailed his performance. Afterward, his only regret was that he didn't have more lines.

I guess we all have a little "ham" in us, a desire to stand out, to be in the spotlight, even if only for one day.

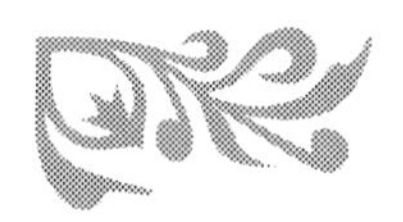

Anybody But the Sisters

As avid tennis fans, one of our greatest pleasures has been to watch the rise of the Williams sisters, Venus and Serena. Almost everyone doubted Richard Williams when he predicted greatness for his two daughters long before their skills warranted it. But Richard had the last laugh. And so did Venus and Serena.

They burst onto the tennis scene in the mid-1990s, all teenage giggles and white hair beads. But when they got onto a tennis court, they played their hearts out. Neil and I would go to see them in person whenever they came to Miami. We would cheer and clap until our voices gave out and our hands practically bled. In one memorable match, Serena was down 4-0 to Martina Hingis, the number one player in the world at the time, when there was a rain delay. When the match resumed, so did our boisterous cheering. Serena upped her game and went on to win the match. "What kept you going?" asked the announcer afterward. "It was those people up there," replied Serena, pointing to us. "I didn't want to let them down." The glow from that remark kept us returning to watch her matches again and again.

We noticed a curious thing about the reaction to "the sisters," as the sports announcers almost invariably and annoyingly refer to them. Between them, Serena and Venus have won numerous Olympic gold medals for the United States, but do not inspire adulation from American fans. Quite the opposite. "Whom are you rooting for?" I once asked a friend on the tennis court at Mystic Pointe. "Anybody but the sisters," she replied. I was shocked. And then I remembered my mother telling me that the men at her assisted living facility had a stock answer when asked whom they were rooting for during major golf tournaments. "ABT. Anybody but Tiger."

As the years went by, Venus and Serena picked up some more fans as they rose in the rankings, becoming number one and two. But the bias against them in Miami was always there. Many fans would root for anyone else, even an obscure Russian named Tatiana, as long as they were white.

We like to think the racial divide in this country is a thing of the past, and then there it is, rearing its ugly head. The division between "us" and "them." Anybody but Tiger. Anybody but the sisters.

Woodstock Unvisited

Before it was a "nation" or a watershed event attracting half-a-million music lovers, Woodstock was just a concert promising three days of peace and music. We knew we could count on Neil's parents for only one day of babysitting our one-year-old, Michael, so we decided to go to the Saturday session. The Who, Janis Joplin, and the Grateful Dead were among the acts scheduled for that day. We purchased two tickets for seven dollars apiece and told Neil's friend, Howie, that we'd meet him there.

We never made it to the concert site. After dropping Michael off in Peekskill, we headed north on Route 17. Eventually we hit total gridlock, parked the car on the side of the road, and began the five-mile trek to the concert grounds. There were many people leaving at this point, warning us of the chaos ahead. Those warnings, plus the fact that my feet were starting to hurt, made me urge Neil to return to our car and head for home. Howie, unencumbered by any offspring or a nagging wife, made it there and stayed for the entire event.

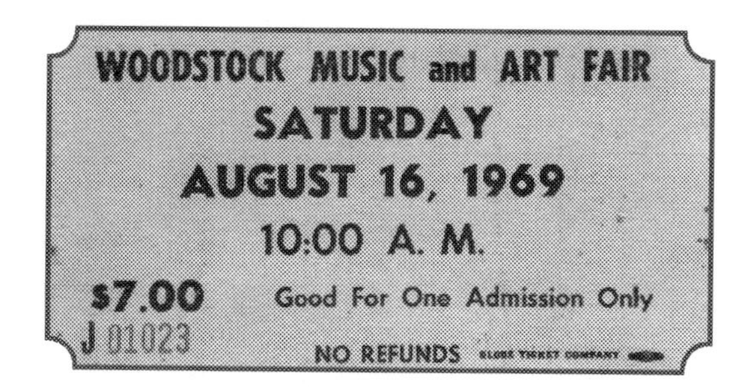

Improbably, we still have our tickets forty-three years later. I framed them several weeks before the house burned down and hung them on a wall in the kitchen. They are one of only half a dozen items to escape the fire unscathed. They hang on the wall of the new kitchen now, a reminder of a more innocent time. A time when a ticket to see the greatest rock-and-roll performers of all time cost a mere seven dollars.

The Guardian

It was my first day at American University in Washington, D.C. and I was beside myself with excitement to be actually living in the city of my dreams. After meeting and sharing dinner with my two assigned roommates, Anna and Susie, I left McDowell Hall and headed downtown by bus to take in the sights of our nation's capital. The way many romantics feel about Paris, that's how I have always regarded Washington.

A.U. girls gather at Anna's 1970 wedding: Lynne, me, Anna, Alice and Fritz

It was a perfect late summer evening and I sat at the front of the bus as it meandered down Massachusetts Avenue, passing all the foreign embassies and the Vice President's mansion near the Naval

Observatory. I struck up a conversation with the middle-aged driver, who was worried about my safety. He could spot a small town girl in the big city from a mile away. He made me promise to meet him at the bus stop at exactly 10 o'clock for the return trip to AU. I spent hours practically dancing down the historic streets and drinking in the sights. The monuments! The Capitol! The White House! Each lit up with a mystical, magical glow. I was in heaven.

I was there waiting as the bus driver pulled up at exactly 10, with a relieved grin on his face. I never stopped talking during the return trip, sharing my excitement with him. His concern made me feel safe and less alone. I like to think my enthusiasm made him look at his route through new eyes. Those of a young girl away from home for the first time, living in the city she had been in love with from afar for so many years.

Turning Fifty

I spent an entire year planning my fiftieth birthday. My husband indulged me in this, relieved to have avoided the arduous task of planning a party, surprise or otherwise.

I decided to go for broke, pulling out all the stops. If I was going to turn half a century, it would be in style and it would be my way. I booked tickets on the Concorde from JFK to Paris. We were able to get tickets for the Wimbledon quarterfinal matches in London. We booked fine hotels in Paris, London and Nice, with a side trip to Monaco. On paper, it looked fabulous.

Of course, the reality was something less. The Concorde was smoky, which gave me a headache, as did the free Mimosas. (Who drinks alcohol at 8 am?) The Paris hotel room was tiny and claustrophobic, barely large enough for the king-sized bed, and the hotel elevator was coffin-sized. On the morning of my actual birthday, we headed for the Ritz Hotel for breakfast and were turned away, as Neil's casual clothing did not begin to meet their high standards.

Nice was lovely, our hotel a converted prison with a breathtaking view of the Mediterranean, not to mention the topless sunbathers staying next door. However, it was there that I read in the Herald Tribune that my favorite tennis player, Monica Seles, had lost in an early round and was out of Wimbledon. I was devastated. As it turned out, it didn't matter because it rained continuously during both our days at Wimbledon. The English accepted this with their usual stiff upper lips, but I was beyond annoyed by the fact that there were no make-up matches. Almost as disappointing was the British version of strawberries and cream. For years I had pictured this as some dreamy, mouth-watering confection. The reality could not have been more different. We are talking clotted unsweetened cream and unripe strawberries! I felt like crying. I spent way too much money on over-priced souvenir sweatshirts to pass the time. Also, because I was freezing. The temperature never rose above fifty degrees and my one turtleneck got a real workout. So much for the darling little sundresses I had packed.

The return trip to the States was uneventful. Less than a week later an Air France flight from JFK to Paris blew up mid-air and Neil vowed to never fly again. And we haven't. Instead we have driven across the country twice, enjoying ourselves immensely. Now that I've lowered my expectations, my birthday celebrations are just fine, usually better than expected. I enjoy a delicious dinner in the company of my favorite person. Who could ask for anything more?

Taking Care of Business

There may be many successful family businesses out there, but speaking from experience, I sincerely doubt it. My father-in-law purchased an ongoing wholesale seafood company in the 1930s, and as his three sons came of age and graduated from college, each went into the family business. They brought along whatever education they had acquired but also some long-held family resentments.

It is hard to grow up when you are closely involved with your siblings every day and have unresolved issues. And let's face it, how many families do not fit that description in some way? Show me a non-dysfunctional family and I'll show you a rarity. As the youngest son, Neil joined the business much later than his brothers, though he had absorbed a lot working there each summer. I don't know of any movies about Fulton Fish Market, but if you watch *Splash*, a favorite of ours, you will get an idea of what a family-run wholesale business is like. The only difference is that, in the case of *Splash*, the business is the fruit and vegetable industry, not seafood. Also, no one at Fulton Fish Market looks like Daryl Hannah, or Tom Hanks, for that matter.

When Neil and I were "keeping company," as his father used to quaintly put it, I'd take a train into Manhattan from New Jersey and meet Neil and his dad for lunch at "Sweet's," a landmark restaurant on Fulton Street, just steps away from the bustling seafood market. Sweet's made a grey sole dish that was sheer poetry, a buttery delight topped with just the right amount of breadcrumbs. I was never a real devotee of fish entrees until I dined there.

The working hours at Fulton Fish Market are the real killer. My husband is by nature not a morning person. In college, he used to schedule his earliest class for noon and he still sometimes missed it. So waking up at three in the morning was not something he ever got used to. The only good thing about it was the easy commute into Manhattan at that hour. There were plenty of cars on the Long Island Expressway but not the bumper-to-bumper traffic experienced during rush hour. The crazy hours took quite a toll, and on many Fridays he would take an afternoon nap and sleep straight through until Saturday morning. I learned early in our marriage not to make any social plans for Friday nights.

In 1983, Neil finally came up with a plan to alleviate the stress of waking up at three a.m. five days a week. Since Wednesday was a very quiet day in his department and most of Fulton Market, he decided to start taking Wednesdays off each week and take a cut in pay. He did this with my blessing and his father's. Unfortunately, his brothers greatly resented it. One went so far as to order in large quantities of a fresh item, live lobsters, on Wednesdays for Neil's department, so they would be dead and cause a problem on Thursdays. The other showed up with his wife at a dinner honoring me for charity work the week after the plan went into effect and walked right past me without a greeting. The workplace in general became filled with tension, and by year's end, Neil came home one day and said, "That's it. I'm leaving." I was flooded with relief.

For the next three years, he was a househusband and I worked full-time in the newspaper business. Neil got to spend lots of quality time with our sons, who were then teenagers. And he got to sleep, sleep as long as he wished, seven days a week. He went food shopping and learned to cook. He'd call me at the office to complain that dinner was on the table and demand to know why I wasn't there. I savored the role reversal.

Unfortunately, in his absence, the business went sharply downhill. So much so that his father developed an ulcer, which almost killed him when it perforated and he was rushed to the hospital for emergency surgery. When he recovered, he took a good look at the state of the business and decided to make major changes. He asked Neil to come back and run the business on his own terms. He made him president, which his brothers did not take well. One walked out the door of his father's house with these parting words. "You always liked Neil best." That brother never saw or spoke to his father or Neil again.

Within six months after Neil took charge, the business was back in the black, which astounded the accountant who had been with my father-in-law since the 1930s. "Bill, I've never seen anything like this," he told him. Twenty-six years later, a lot has changed, including a move to the Bronx from lower Manhattan for the entire Fulton Fish Market. But business is still good, although some weeks are better than others. My husband may look like a rock musician, but he definitely inherited his father's head for business. That and his degree in psychology have made him a formidable company C.E.O. His success surprised a lot of people but I wasn't one of them. I always knew he had it in him to be successful in whatever he did, as long as he could do things his own way.

The Sound of Silence

Deafness is usually diagnosed quite early in life, but hearing loss is quite different. Mine was not officially diagnosed until I was in my thirties and working in the newspaper business. I published an article about free hearing tests at a nearby college and decided to go have myself checked out. I was not really surprised to learn that I had a high frequency hearing loss in both ears. I had felt for years that I was missing words and even sounds that everyone else seemed to hear. All my life, I instinctively chose seats at the front of classrooms. It didn't matter in churches, as I never listened to a sermon, not a one, using the time to daydream instead.

As a college student many years ago, I was conducting research for a term paper at the National Library of Congress and was completely unaware that Neil and two friends had sat down alongside me. I attributed it to my intense concentration but it is certainly possible that I just didn't hear them. When I was newly pregnant and visiting my obstetrician for the first time, I didn't hear her call out "Mrs. Smith" the first few times. "It must be a very new name," she said with a smirk as I signed myself in. Not really. I just hadn't heard her until she raised her voice a notch.

As a journalist covering meetings and interviewing subjects for a living, I needed to have all the help I could get. So following the diagnosis, the quest for the perfect hearing aid began. Every five years or so, improvements are made and I get the new, improved model. This year, I finally listened to the experts and ordered two aids, one for each ear, which is, as promised, a vast improvement. But I know that even with the aids, my hearing is less than optimal. Plus a lifetime of sub-par hearing has made me into a poor listener. I have always preferred to get information by reading rather than hearing. Closed captioning is a boon for people like me. Many times I have wished that all of life could be closed-captioned.

Sometimes I wonder what I would do if I found out that a simple surgical procedure could correct my hearing loss. And then I think of the mornings before I leave the house or apartment and how I revel in the sound of silence as I read the newspapers, browse the Internet or write my memoirs. My last action as I leave home is to put my hearing aids in and the silence is immediately swallowed up by the cacophony of everyday life. It sounds like an oxymoron, but the sound of silence can indeed be a wonderful thing in this noisy modern world.

Sentimental Journey

The invitation arrived in the spring of 1989. The 25th reunion of Glen Rock High School's class of 1964 would be held in Tenafly, New Jersey in early October. Should I go? There was only one answer and, besides, I had four months to lose weight, shop for the perfect outfit, and study the yearbook to bone up on names and faces.

On the appointed day, I slipped a cassette of sixties tunes into the car stereo and headed over the George Washington Bridge, crossing over into my own personal "Twilight Zone." I was breathless from a combination of anticipation and dread. My husband had offered to accompany me, but seemed relieved when I insisted he stay home. Upon arrival, I took a deep breath then wandered into what appeared to be a vast sea of couples. I began to seriously regret having left my human security blanket home. I affixed the nametag complete with the dreadful graduation photo to my designer duds. I began to circulate the room like the self-confident grown-up I had become.

Then it was time to sit down to dinner and for one horrible moment, the fancy restaurant was transformed into the high school cafeteria and I had no one to sit with. I felt all the self-assurance of that doe-eyed teenager plastered to my bosom. Panic subsided as I found my way to an empty seat at a table of friendly faces. The next three hours passed by in a blur. Amid the usual cocktail party chitchat were mild flirtations with boys (now men) that I had once admired from afar, juicy exchanges of gossip, teary reminiscences about classmates who had died, and a few revelations of startlingly personal details of our now-complicated lives. The noise level of the room rose as it filled with squeals, giggles and shrieks more befitting a high school corridor than a room full of forty-somethings.

It turned out that we really needed nametags, as more than a few people were now unrecognizable. There was a general consensus that the women looked great, but the men, with a few notable exceptions, had not aged as well. In fact, they looked more like our fathers than our contemporaries. However, the cheerleaders were instantly recognizable. They looked almost exactly the same as in high school, right down to the hairstyles. They had discovered their look early on and were sticking with it, while the rest of us had spent twenty-five years desperately trying to look as unlike our high school selves as possible.

Linda, Sally, me, Carole, and Alice (note the crimped hair)

By evening's end, I knew why I felt compelled to go. For the previous 25 years, while others debated whether life began at birth or conception, I had maintained that my life began at high school graduation. My *Wonder Years* seemed far removed from the wife and mother, feminist and journalist that I had become. But in reality, the person I was in high school is very much a part of the person I am today. The experiences of high school, both good and bad, helped shape me. I guess a lot of my classmates felt the same way. They came from as far away as Texas and California, while, interestingly, many living nearby chose to skip the reunion. And I can understand that, too. It took a lot of courage to walk through that door and face those twin high school demons of rejection and ridicule. At mid-life, confronting the past can be even more terrifying than facing the future.

I arrived home exhausted and drained of all emotion. "How was it?" my husband wanted to know. It took me a moment to come up with the appropriate word. "Mind-boggling," I replied. "But I wouldn't have missed it for the world."

Scout's Honor

Back in the 1950s, I was a member of the Girl Scouts of America. I don't remember making a conscious decision to join. I guess it was just something girls of that era did, at least those in Glen Rock, New Jersey. The uniforms were ugly. (Green is definitely not my color.) The cookies were overpriced to say the least. And what was the deal with those badges? After you "earned" your badge, you then had to sew it onto those sashes, which were just as ugly as the uniforms they adorned.

My girl scouting experiences were memorable on only a few occasions. It was during one scouting event, a play of some sort, that I got my first period. (Previous generations referred to this female monthly imposition as "the curse" or "my friend." We just called it "my period.") This resulted in an awkward conversation with my mother and the hasty acquisition of the necessary supplies. I was twelve, about average age, but apparently my mother was surprised at the timing. Unlike some of my friends, there was no celebration of my official entry into womanhood.

A second scouting event was our troop's visit to an institution for the mentally retarded. I remember feeling extremely uncomfortable at all the unfamiliar sights and sounds, and so sorry for "Joanie," whose younger sister lived there. Her cheeks burned a bright scarlet the entire time of our visit. I think we were all relieved to return to the "normality" of our everyday lives, but especially Joan.

My third scouting memory was of a camping trip to Nancy's backyard, where tents had been erected. Shortly after I laid down on the damp, hard ground inside my tent, I vomited, which sent my fellow tent mates running for their lives. I ended up spending the night in the family's lovely guest room, happily ensconced on a soft mattress under a lacy duvet, Nancy's mom at my beck and call. It was heaven!

Before our marriage, Neil mentioned several times of his desire to buy a camper and travel the country. I would roll my eyes and bite my tongue. It would be more than three decades before we finally got around to a cross-country trip. When we did, in 1999, there was no camper in tow. We drove across America in our BMW, staying mainly at four-star hotels with room service, of course. The lessons of my years as a Girl Scout camper were not lost on this Glen Rock girl.

Leaving Winter Behind

I have always hated winter. I don't ski, I can't ice skate and I hate being cold. When my kids were little, I dreaded putting on their snowsuits, boots, mittens and other cold weather paraphernalia. Only to repeat the whole process the next day, and the one after that. And, most of all, particularly as I got older, the thought of driving on icy roads terrified me. Spring meant renewal, summer was sheer bliss, and fall at least treated your senses to the breath-taking colors of the turning leaves. But winter held zero charm for me. Luckily, Neil felt pretty much the same way, and each winter we looked forward to our three-week vacation in sunny Florida to escape the bleakness of January in New York.

In 1987, the year before our youngest son graduated from high school, we put a deposit down on a new condominium in Aventura, Florida. The following August, my husband and I flew from our home in New York for the closing. We were intrigued by the development's exotic sounding name, Mystic Pointe, and the fact that my father-in-law lived within walking distance was a big plus. We looked forward to tropical breezes instead of shoveling snow. But as lifelong North Easterners, we were a bit apprehensive. Would we enjoy condo living? What would our neighbors be like? Did we do the right thing?

After the closing, we went out for Chinese food. At the end of the meal, out came the orange slices and fortune cookies. As is my custom, I read my fortune out loud: "In the land of hope there is no winter." Neil and I looked at each other gleefully. We had done the right thing!

"Martha Stewart Doesn't Live Here"

I used to hang a small plaque in the kitchen of our Florida condominium that read "Martha Stewart Doesn't Live Here." It had a practical use, too. Because it was essentially a framed hand-painted tile, it could be used on the dining room table under hot casserole dishes. It was very dual-purpose, in a Martha Stewart sort of way. But I rarely used it for that. It was more of a statement, one which women usually understood and men didn't.

Many women of my generation, including me, grew up striving hard to be "perfect." The perfect daughter. The perfect wife. The perfect mother. The perfect homemaker. That's a whole lot of perfects, and it is easy to lose sight of who you really are in the pursuit of all that perfection. So at a certain point in our lives, most of us wisely gave up that impossible and frustrating quest and learned to settle for being something less than perfect but truer to who we really were. We learned to be satisfied with being "good enough." And along the way, we learned how to laugh at ourselves when things didn't turn out as planned. We learned how to make the best of things and find joy in unexpected places. And when a perfect moment came along, usually unexpectedly and in ways beyond our control, we learned to savor it. Not because we made it happen but because it happened at all.

When Martha Stewart's life imploded in 2004, I took the plaque down. I wasn't going to pile onto her when she was down. And, anyway, it was never meant to be an anti-Martha Stewart statement. It was a statement of liberation, of freedom from obsessing about the need to be perfect in all things.

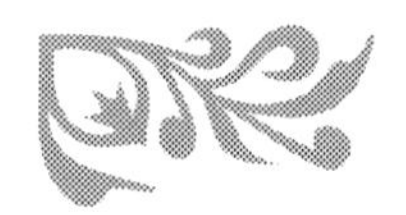

Ed Sullivan

If you grew up in the 1950s, chances are that every Sunday night your family gathered around the television set to watch the *Ed Sullivan Show* on CBS. Ed Sullivan always tried to have something for every member of the family on his "variety" show. He had comedians, he had rock and roll stars, he had jugglers, he had live animal acts, and, for reasons unknown, he had Topo Gigio.

I vividly remember the first time I saw Elvis Presley. We were staying at my grandparents' home in Dover, Delaware. The television was tuned in to the Ed Sullivan Show when Elvis made his entrance. I was ten at the time and was fascinated by this utterly unique entertainer. He started with two ballads, "Love Me Tender" and "Don't Be Cruel." Later in the show, he returned and let loose with a hip-swiveling rendition of "Hound Dog." I recall our elders behind us harrumphing their disapproval, which only caused Elvis to seem even more desirable to Marci and me. Our family was not alone. More than sixty million viewers watched that broadcast. Upwards of eighty percent of all American televisions were tuned in for this particular show.

Fast forward to 1967, when Neil and I spent our wedding night with Ed Sullivan. Let me rephrase. We spent our wedding night at the New York Hilton in Manhattan. Ed Sullivan was a few blocks away at the headquarters of CBS-TV. The Lovin' Spoonful were among his musical guests that evening, an act we didn't want to miss. So after hurriedly "consummating" our marriage, we turned on the television at 8 pm to catch their performance. Just before they came on, there was a discreet knock on the door. The maid wanted to know if all was in order and we needed anything. She seemed flustered by the sight of the unmade bed. We assured her that all was fine, took the mints and sent her on her way. Then we sat back to watch the show.

Years went by and we saw Ed Sullivan again, this time in person at Yonkers Raceway. The announcer introduced Ed and the crowd booed loudly. It was Ed's turn to look flustered. He was obviously stunned by the crowd's reaction. I wanted to take him aside and assure him that it wasn't personal. Racetrack aficionados would boo Mother Teresa herself if you let them.

Sour Grapes

The human body is a mysterious thing. We take good health for granted until the day our body betrays us.

It started with a bump below the surface of the skin on the back of my right shoulder. There was no pain but it felt strange to the touch, like a marble under the skin. "A cyst," declared my primary care physician. But since my sister Marci had been diagnosed with melanoma the year before, I insisted that the situation be explored further.

I was referred to a dermatologist. "A cyst," he declared firmly. "But I can remove it if you insist." I insisted. "Oh," he exclaimed in surprise after making an incision. "It's not a cyst. I'll send it to a lab for a biopsy and we'll call with the results."

I should have known the news was not good when the nurse insisted I come in person for the lab results. "Cancer," said the doctor in a matter-of-fact way. "You need to see a surgeon and have it removed." That was the end of the discussion. Not even a pat on the shoulder.

I drove home in a fog, grimly concentrating on the road ahead to keep my mind off the news. I found a song on my CD player, "Sour Grapes" by John Prine, that I found oddly reassuring. I would sing along, then press the replay button again and again as I made my way south on I-95 and east on Ives Dairy Road. I could keep it together as long as I could sing along with John Prine.

"Sour grapes. You can laugh and stare. Sour grapes. I don't care."

The Cancer Club

It happened on a cross-country trip in the summer of 2000. Neil and I were returning from a family reunion in San Diego, which was highlighted by my brother's wedding to his second wife, Elisabeth. One of our final stops was Cleveland, Ohio, home of the Rock and Roll Hall of Fame. We spent a glorious day there, reveling in all things rock and roll. At least, I did. For Neil, the visit was marred by a trip to the men's room. The sight of his urine, which was the color of pink lemonade instead of the usual pale yellow, upset him, but like most long-married couples, he didn't mention it to me until we left the building. He hadn't wanted to spoil the day for me. As a result, I have fond memories of our trip to that magical place alongside Lake Erie and recommend it highly to all my friends who, like me, grew up reveling in the sounds of our generation's music. Neil remembers it differently, as the beginning of his eventual entry into the Cancer Club.

When we arrived in New York, the doctor visits began. From the first visit, we knew that cancer was a possibility, but we were hoping for a diagnosis of a urinary infection or something less frightening. An MRI of Neil's bladder clearly showed a tumor. We turned to our longtime friend and neighbor, Freddy Kunken, for a recommendation for a top urologist and we were able to see him without delay. He reassured us and explained that Neil's was the "good kind" of bladder cancer, likening it to a stalk of broccoli. (It would be years before I could look at broccoli and not think of cancer.) Surgery was scheduled and performed at North Shore Hospital in Manhasset. Neil's last words to Dr. Waldbaum were, "Doc, my sex life is very important to me."

I waited anxiously while Neil went "under the knife," and shortly afterward, the doctor came out to tell me all had gone well and Neil was now cancer-free. He had the "good" kind of bladder cancer, the kind that was confined to the tumor and had not spread to the walls or beyond. As a result, he would not need chemotherapy or radiation. It is twelve years later and there has been no reoccurrence, but the experience changed both of us. When he voted for Ralph Nader instead of Al Gore that November, I swallowed my fury and chalked it up to post-traumatic stress disorder from the whole cancer experience.

Just a few years later, I underwent my first cancer scare when a routine mammogram showed what appeared to be a tumor in my left breast. Because my mother was a two-time survivor of breast cancer, I was not my usual optimistic self while undergoing the needle core biopsy and awaiting the results. I was a wreck, but held off telling my mother about the ordeal until it was over and the tumor proved to be benign. I would not be joining Neil as a member of the Cancer Club.

My sister Marci was diagnosed with melanoma shortly after this, but her treatment went well and she has had no reoccurrence. However, her experience made me more vigilant than I might have been, and when I felt a bump under the skin of my right shoulder, I began my own doctor rounds. It turns out that I had a very rare form of cancer, dermata fibroid carcinoma protuberans. It was confined to the soft tissue instead of the bone, so a simple but wide excision could remove it completely. "You are very lucky," the oncologist intoned solemnly. He was right, though at the time I was feeling anything but lucky. I have a large, ugly scar on the back of my shoulder that bears witness to my ordeal. It looks like the aftermath of an attack by some ferocious animal. Oddly, Marci's melanoma scar is on the back of her right shoulder, too.

And so, I joined Neil and Marci and my mom and millions of others in the Cancer Club. We are the cancer survivors. We take one day at a time and nothing for granted. We have good days and bad days. Days when we feel lucky for having had the "good kind" of our cancers. Days when we fear our bodies are going to betray us again. Good days and bad. Ups and downs. Kind of like life in general.

R-E-S-P-E-C-T

What is the one ingredient without which no marriage can thrive? Ask Aretha Franklin. It is respect. It is the foundation upon which any good marriage must be built. But in actuality, all relationships need respect to survive and thrive. Relationships between parents and children of all ages. Relationships between in-laws.

Feminism was built on the desire, even need, of women to be respected by men and other women. In so many societies, women were, and still are in some cases, considered to be inferior to men. That is what the fight for equality between the sexes was and is all about. Not just equal pay but equal value. When men's opinions are valued over women's, simply because they belong to men, there can be no equality. It is hard to believe that women didn't even have the right to vote in this country, this so-called democracy, until our Constitution was amended in 1920. For all those years, it was assumed and rarely challenged, that women's votes would be the same as their husbands. And, of course, that the opinions of unmarried women were totally irrelevant.

Feminism had so many myths about it from the start. Women were trying to become men. Ugly women were banding together because no man would have them. Women wanted to reject all traditional roles, including motherhood and homemaking.

Gloria Steinem did more to change people's perceptions of the movement than anyone else. Through the years I would drag friends to hear her speak in person and their first comment was always, "She's so pretty!" As if being attractive and a feminist were irreconcilable. But to me, her most attractive traits were always her keen intellect and the ability to make her points intelligently and calmly, the total opposite of the angry feminist prototype the media loved to portray. She has been at the forefront all these years, fighting for the rights younger women now take for granted. Earning respect, not just demanding it.

I rarely lose my temper, but when I do, it is generally because someone has disrespected me unfairly with a wave of a hand or a snide look. Then, watch out! Hell hath no fury like a disrespected feminist.

On the Inside Looking Out

A great fantasy for a Bloomingdale's aficionado might be to spend hours inside the store, unbothered by crowds or salespeople. It happened to me once upon a time. And all I can say is, be careful what you wish for.

It was in the late 1980s and we traveled into Manhattan so that Neil and his father could have a business dinner meeting with some bank representatives. I was invited to join them for a drink, after which I made myself scarce so the "men" could talk business. No problem. I headed for Bloomingdale's on the Upper East Side and its children's department, a favorite haunt of mine. The wife of one of Neil's salesmen had just given birth to a baby girl, so I spent about an hour wandering the aisles, looking for the perfect baby gift. As the mother of sons, I always take great delight in shopping for little girls. Mission accomplished, I began looking for a salesperson to ring up my purchase. There were none in sight. And then it began to slowly dawn upon me that there were no customers either. The only apparent movement was the down escalator, so I reluctantly put aside the carefully chosen gift and began the descent to the ground level.

At this point, I began talking to myself, just to break the eerie silence. The ground floor was as empty as the rest of the store. I tried to exit onto Lexington Avenue but the doors were securely locked. Passing pedestrians spotted me and waved as if I were some kind of live window shop display. I tried to give them a distress signal of some sort, then gave up and waved back. How I wished I were on the outside looking in instead of the other way around. For some reason, colorful strobe lights were crisscrossing the store, adding to the surreal quality of the scene. I expected guard dogs to appear at any minute to take care of any trespassers. My imagination was really running wild as the adrenaline began pumping.

Finally, I spotted some people in the far distance, employees silently heading out a special exit. I joined them, and then fled the scene, heading for the nearest cafe where I collapsed into a heap. When I met up with Neil an hour later, I asked how the meeting had gone. I waited patiently as he described it in detail. "How was your evening?" he asked finally. "It was a nightmare," I told him shakily. "A nightmare." I regaled him with all the details on the way home to Long Island.

Mirror, Mirror

Our home on Long Island is smack in the middle of the famed Gold Coast. Across the fence to the south of our property is an estate, once owned by Mary and Laddie Sanford. It was there that they wined and dined the Duke and Duchess of Windsor, with Duke Ellington providing entertainment on the grand piano. When Mary Sanford sold the estate shortly after we moved into our home in 1977, Christie's held an auction of its contents under a giant white tent on the property. I dragged Neil there, determined to leave with a piece of history.

It came in the form of a mirror, a quite large mirror, measuring three feet across and almost five feet high. The frame was wooden and elaborately carved with figures of animals and people, even a king. I had to have it, and, as it turned out, mine was the winning bid. I was giddy with excitement as we ferried it home and hung it on our dining room wall.

We lost almost everything in the fire during the summer of 2009, but the mirror somehow survived. It smelled of smoke and the finish had melted a bit, but the mirror remained unbroken, the frame intact. I made some calls, then schlepped it to Locust Valley, leaving it for the winter with two respected furniture restorers. When we returned the following June, I retrieved it and was delighted with the job. It was truly even better than before the fire. I planned the dining room of the new house around the mirror, having the new furniture finished in the same rich dark brown hue.

I gaze upon it almost every day, thrilled to have something old in my brand new house. An object of beauty, true, but also one of history. A reminder of Long Island's glory days.

Mistletoe and Melancholy

As a child, I was an enthusiastic participant in all things Christmas. I loved decorating the Christmas tree, particularly with old ornaments that we had collected through the years. I loved going Christmas caroling, even though I had a terrible singing voice. I loved choosing gifts carefully and the wrapping and unwrapping rituals that went along with gift giving. I always considered Christmas to be my half-birthday, since my actual birthday was June 25th, exactly half a year earlier. A perfect setup for getting gifts every six months!

When I converted to Judaism in 1967, I never considered how I would feel when the first Christmas rolled around. It was a strange and sad and confusing time, made even worse by the death of my best friend the month before. I'm sure I'm not the only convert to Judaism who feels somewhat conflicted about Christmas. It comes with the territory.

When the kids came along, we eventually found ourselves celebrating both Hanukkah and Christmas, since, despite my conversion to Judaism, my half of the family was still Christian. We didn't have a Christmas tree in our house but my parents did, and we would visit on Christmas Day and exchange gifts. I didn't realize how unusual this was until I overheard Michael bragging to a playmate that he was lucky. He got gifts for both Christmas and all eight days of Hanukkah. The playmate looked crestfallen.

I'm older now but still feel conflicted when the December holidays come around. I always gain more than a few pounds, compulsively stuffing my face with holiday goodies as if to fill up the hole I feel inside from the loss of holidays past. It has nothing to do with religion, but everything to do with family traditions and childhood memories, and, of course, the family members who are no longer with us.

You can't erase your past or your memories. They are a part of what makes you who you are. You can't un-memorize all the Christmas carols you learned by heart at an early age. And so I throw myself into holiday activities at the condo, organizing the Christmas tree lighting party and making latkes for the Hanukkah party, trying to have it both ways. "Happy holidays," I tell my neighbors with all the cheer I can muster. But deep down all I really feel is melancholy. Not a longing for the good old days, but rather a wish for the time when life was a little less complicated. When my young heart was filled with the simple but profound feelings of comfort and joy, whole-heartedly celebrating the holiday season with the people I loved.

Oy Vey!

The expression "shiksa goddess" has popped up in our culture through the years. It was probably Lenny Bruce who first used it, but it was picked up by other comedians and was even the subject of a short story by the late, brilliant playwright/author Wendy Wasserstein. Despite my conversion to Judaism, my father-in-law used to occasionally refer to me jokingly as a "shiksa." Then came the day when I read, with genuine horror, that the literal translation of the word "shiksa" is "abomination." I felt sick to my stomach. When I told him this, he quietly absorbed the information. He never used the word again.

There are many Yiddish words that have become part of everyday language in American life, at least in the places we live in. Schmuck, for instance, is a commonly used expression nowadays for an idiot. However, the literal translation is penis. When Neil and I got engaged in the summer of 1966, we decided that the families would meet in Peekskill for a casual get-together, instead of a big engagement party. The adults were gathered at a large picnic table while Neil's young nieces and nephews played nearby. At one point my mother asked innocently, "What is a schmuck?" A very long silence ensued. Then Neil's father came up with the perfect answer. "Well, Ruth," he replied. "It's the best part of a man." My poor mother turned twelve shades of red, but the rest of us laughed heartily, and the conversation resumed.

My favorite Yiddish word is "makheteneste." It means your son or daughter's mother-in-law. Makheteneste is a mouthful, but so much easier than saying my son's mother-in-law every time you mention your grandchild's other grandmother. The equivalent expression for your child's father-in-law is "machuten." For some reason this expression is heard much less often than makheteneste. Probably for the same reason that Huey Lewis and the News had a hit song called "Mother-in-Law" but none called "Father-in-Law."

Here's a list of just some of the Yiddish words that have become part of the English language. See how many you can define, especially if you didn't grow up in a house where Yiddish was commonly spoken. Extra points given if you didn't grow up in the New York City area. Mensch, mitzvah, shlep, shlock, schnoz, nosh, dreck, kibitz, klutz, schvitz, chutzpah, goniff, schemata, schmooze, plotz, maven, kvetch, tchotchkes, bubelah, ghetto, glitch, kibosh, zaftig, shmeer, nebbish.

All of these words and many more have enriched our culture. They are frequently mispronounced (Just Google Michele Bachman for her unique take on chutzpah. It's priceless). They are part of what we mean when we talk about America as a melting pot.

Looking Jewish

When I converted to Judaism in 1967, it never occurred to me that I wouldn't look the part. After all, the Jewish people I knew didn't have a common "look," so I expected to fit right in. Early in our marriage, we were invited to a party at Neil's brother's house. I purchased a pair of cranberry velvet "hot pants" for the occasion, along with a matching blouse. It must have been the latest fad because another guest wore virtually the same outfit.

During the evening, a discussion ensued about the composition of my brother-in-law's neighborhood in East Hills. "It's about 80/20," declared one man. "Which is okay, but if it goes to 70/30, we'll look to move." My husband, usually quite laid-back, pounced. "80/20 what? What are you talking about? Animals?" There was total silence for one very long minute. The neighbor's comeback: "I thought your wife didn't look Jewish." We left soon after but not before my sister-in-law tearfully confessed in the kitchen that she would rather that her son marry someone like me than our other sister-in-law, who was born Jewish. This was not much of a compliment since at the time there was no love lost between them. Needless to say, we were not invited back to any more of their neighborhood gatherings. Not that we would have gone.

This was not my first encounter with the "looking Jewish" conundrum. When we moved to our first home in Westbury, I introduced myself to our elderly next-door neighbor. The subject of religion arose, and I mentioned casually that we were Jewish. When she told me I didn't look Jewish, I quickly replied, "Neither do you."

She took this as a compliment, blushing slightly and primping her red hair.

Years later, the wife of one of Neil's cousins was bragging about her son-in-law. "He is not only successful financially, but very good looking for a Jewish man." I could not believe my ears and told her so. From anyone else, this would be considered an anti-Semitic remark. She had the grace to look embarrassed.

More recently, I was reading a book about memoir writing by my good friend, Sue William Silverman, and came across a passage about her high school years. She and my best friend Kathy were dating the same classmate, a boy named Jamie, and Sue remembers wishing fervently that she could change her looks and become more like "Christian Kathy." This was a shock to my senses as the teenager I remember was very attractive, as well as an honor student and member of the "in" crowd.

I'm still not sure of what "looking Jewish" is. But when a neighbor in our condo was describing a Weight Watchers leader to me recently and said, "She looks a lot like you, Paula. A middle-aged Jewish woman," I was thrilled. I took it as the highest possible compliment. It took me over forty years but I had made it!

In Praise of Porches

There is something quite wonderful about a house with a porch. They used to be a common feature on almost all houses, but somehow fell out of favor in modern times. For many years my family owned a cottage on Caspian Lake in Vermont built in 1910, where we spent our childhood summers, and the large front porch overlooking the lake was a favorite spot for playing games and reading. At my grandparents' house in Dover, Delaware, my sister and I would sleep on the second floor porch overlooking the formal boxwood gardens, falling asleep to the soothing sound of crickets.

When central air conditioning came along, people started enclosing their porches and new homes were built without them. But whenever I spotted an older house with wrap-around porches, usually in Oyster Bay or Bayville, I envied the owners. And when we stayed on the Biltmore Estate in Asheville, N.C., or at other grand hotels, I inevitably found myself drawn to a rocking chair on one of the porches every morning.

After our Long Island home was destroyed by fire in 2009, we met with a local architect with intentions to just rebuild the same house on the site. "Can I tweak things a bit?" asked our architect, Brian Shore, with a twinkle in his eye. "Sure," we replied, figuring we had nothing to lose. I literally gasped when the first drawings arrived. Our plain 1950s-style ranch had been transformed into a house with charm. A house with sky-lit porches integrated into the design. A front porch off the laundry room. A rear porch off the dining room, overlooking the pool and gardens. Even a side porch off Mike's bedroom, with a ramp for easy egress.

There are other changes Brian made to the house, including a grander entrance, higher ceilings and larger windows. But the porches remain my favorite feature. I greet the mornings in a wicker rocking chair on the sun-filled front porch armed with a cup of coffee and the daily newspapers. In the afternoon, I retire to a chaise lounge on the rear porch with a book. Even on rainy days, a porch is a perfect retreat, the roof serving as a giant umbrella. And when our grandson visits, he stays in Mike's room and spends an inordinate amount of time calling his friends or texting them from a chair on the side porch.

Should we ever have occasion to build another home, my first priority will be the porches. They add something special to a home, a space that is neither indoors nor outdoors but something in between that is uniquely itself. It's an ideal spot for daydreaming or reading or just enjoying life in general.

The Retreat

After my father-in-law died in 1998, his apartment in Turnberry Isle was sold and we moved his furniture into an apartment in our building that we owned but were no longer occupying. It became a kind of shrine to him and I would retreat to it in times of stress. A peaceful place to get away from it all.

Them came the visitors. A trickle at first, then a deluge. We hosted a few boisterous Mack family reunions there. Close friends would visit with their young children, and the door was always open for Neil's employees at Fulton Fish Market. I was kept busy arranging for airport pick-ups and drop-offs and shopping for groceries. (Helpful hint: Ben and Jerry's "Phish Food" never makes it past the first day.)

One problem guest (a relative who shall remain unnamed) came for a week and stayed for three months. Another visitor left behind pink Play Dough embedded in the Oriental rug in the living room, which required a toothbrush and some careful scrubbing on my part to remove. On another occasion, the complaint was that I had only supplied a dozen eggs when clearly more were needed! Then there were the tag-a-long guests. I thought the worst was the vegan who required a detailed description of every item on the menu when we went out to dinner. She was topped the following year by a puppy brought by our friends, despite the fact that I had clearly stated that our condo's policy is that guests are not allowed to bring dogs. Ever. After the puppy peed and defecated on our marble floor during the first hour, our guests quickly departed for grandma's condo nearby. Luckily, the friendship survived.

But along the way, we've also had some stellar guests. One left a lovely hand-written note and a basket of homemade treats. Another arranged to pick up the check ahead of time when the entire family went out for Chinese food. A good friend sat in the audience at the first board meeting I ran as president, beaming her approval. Then there was the cousin's daughter who prepared a home-cooked dinner for Mike and Will during our absence one summer.

The guest apartment gets a lot less use now. I use it for mah jongg games twice a week and it is still the place I go to when I need to get away from it all. Just three floors down but a whole other world.

Hello in There

I adored my paternal grandparents, who were in their mid-sixties when I was born and were very much a part of our young lives. Luckily, they lived to be 86 and 90. I was brought up to respect, admire and obey members of the older generation. Not just my grandparents, but my great aunts and other senior citizens as well.

When I became an adult, I was truly surprised by the disrespect so many members of my generation felt toward the elderly. This ageism is just appalling. If we are lucky, we will all be old some day. It's a stage of life, not a disease. I have many friends who are considerably older than me, and I value their friendship, their wisdom and their different perspectives. Knowing them has enriched my life immeasurably. I study them as possible role models, should I be lucky enough to live into my late eighties and beyond, with my mind and dignity intact.

At the age of twenty-five, singer/song writer John Prine, now sixty-five, wrote and performed a song called "Hello in There." I first heard it at a Bette Midler concert and it affected me deeply. Basically, the chorus goes, "Old trees just grow stronger, and old rivers grow wilder every day. But old people just grow lonesome, waiting for someone to say, Hello in there. Hello..."

I'd love to know what inspired this young songwriter to create this poignant and moving song. Maybe he was lucky and had a special relationship with his grandparents, too. Or maybe he was just smarter and more empathetic than his contemporaries. Either way, hats off to John Prine for making us think and feel compassion for our elderly relatives, friends and neighbors. He may not know what a mensch is, but John Prine is a true mensch.

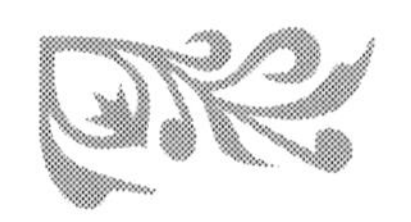

Give Me a Head With Hair

What gives with us and our obsession with our hair? "We are our hair," declared a friend years ago to which I could only reply, "Amen." If it's naturally curly, we want it straight. If it's brown, we want it blonde or red or some other hue. A bad haircut or dye job can reduce a grown woman to tears. I know this from personal experience.

Back in the late 1960s, there was a hit show on Broadway called *Hair.* We went to see it during its first run and really enjoyed it. It was edgy and exhilarating. When we went back to see the revival three years ago, it seemed dated. You see, even a show about hair can be a disappointment.

On our wedding day in 1967, I was a brunette and Neil was clean-shaven and had short dark hair. By the mid-1970s, I had blonde highlights and Neil had a beard and long hair. Forty years later, I still have blonde highlights and, though now mostly gray, Neil's hair is still long, though he wears it in a ponytail. A long, somewhat unkempt ponytail, which looks as if his hair is trying desperately to escape the elastic band enclosing it.

I went through a phase of crimping my hair. Unfortunately, I did it on special occasions, so there are photos to document this inexplicable choice. My twenty-fifth high school reunion. My father-in-law's eightieth-birthday celebration. A family reunion on Long Island. At the reunion, my sister Marci took one look and said dryly, "I hope it isn't permanent." It hurt my feelings at the time, but looking back, she had a point.

Now we watch from the sidelines as our grandson tries to decide on a hairstyle that fits his personality. Recently he went from long flowing locks, which I call the surfer dude look, to a spiky short "do," for which I have no name. He recently posted a photo on Facebook of his latest haircut. He looks miserable in the photo. I know exactly how he feels.

Flashing Lights in the Rear View Mirror

There's nothing else quite like that sickening feeling in the pit of your stomach in response to the sight of flashing lights in your rear view mirror. I am embarrassed to admit that I have experienced this more times than I should have in my almost fifty years of driving. I'm not the champion in the family in this respect, however. Neil has amassed by far the most citations.

During one memorable vacation trip to Florida from New York, he collected a total of five speeding tickets along the way up and down I-95. In South Carolina, the same state trooper stopped him in both directions. He remembered us and greeted us heartily with "How was your trip?" in his Southern drawl. We laughed all the way to the hotel. Neil was stopped in California going more than 100 miles an hour on a virtually empty freeway (I had my nose in a book, totally oblivious to the situation). A helicopter had spotted us from the sky and alerted the highway patrol. In Georgia, on the way to my mom's funeral, Neil received not one but two citations on a back route near Savannah. We were stopped in upstate New York en route to a family reunion in Vermont. (My niece Emily was in the car for this one and considered it a highlight of the reunion.) We were once stopped in Nebraska not for speeding but for leaving a gas station without paying for the gas we had supposedly put in our car. As it turns out, we had stopped at the station to accommodate my need for a bathroom break and Neil had used the time to wash the windshield. The officer took our videotaped statements in the back of his squad car, finally letting us go after concluding we were "in the wrong place at the wrong time." Nothing like some quality time in a police car to spice up your cross-country trip!

My own brushes with "the law" started on the day of my best friend's wedding in 1964. I was rushing around, hair in giant rollers (it was the sixties and flips were the "in" look) when I accidentally went through a red traffic light. Luckily, no collision occurred, but a police officer on the scene pulled me over. After I explained my nervousness about serving as Kathy's maid of honor, he let me go with a gentle warning to pay more attention in the future. Yes, sir!

My second traffic stop was in Flushing, New York, shortly after we moved to Jackson Heights from Washington, D.C. I found myself heading in the wrong direction on Northern Boulevard and panicked, making a U-turn right in front of a giant sign saying "NO U-TURNS." This time two officers pulled me over. The rookie approached me and asked me to show him my license and registration. I explained that I had mailed my New Jersey license in to exchange it for a New York one and had not yet received the new one. He checked with his partner, then came back to ask for the registration. I explained that it was a company car and the registration was in the office at Fulton Fish Market. Another trip back to the squad car. Finally, he returned and told me he could either arrest me or let me go. "You have an honest face, so I'll let you go," he told me as relief flooded my body. I passed that sign numerous times in the four years we lived in Queens, each time wondering how I had missed it and thanking my lucky stars for my "honest-looking" face.

Since then, I have been stopped for speeding on more occasions than I can count, both on Long Island and in Florida. What can I say? I must have a heavy foot. Occasionally, I fight the ticket in court, winning when the officer fails to show. I gave my last citation to a "ticket clinic" that I found on the Internet. It got the fine drastically reduced with no points on my license. Believe it or not, I'm a safe driver, never having been involved in an accident. And I never speed when I have passengers in the car. But as I travel alone, my heavy foot and the "need for speed" get me into trouble from time to time. I see those flashing lights and take a deep breath, pulling over to await my fate, license and registration at the ready.

Egg on My Face

Before her haunting rendition of John Prine's "Hello In There," Bette Midler tells a story about seeing an elderly woman walking on the streets of New York City with a fried egg on her head. People just passed her by as if she and the fried egg were invisible or just part on the "normal" scenery in Manhattan. On a visit to Toronto one summer, I ended up with an egg on my face, too, but mine wasn't fried.

Neil and I were enjoying an excellent meal at a Chinese restaurant. After we finished, I headed for the ladies' room. When I tried to exit the stall, the door was stuck firmly shut. I pulled on it as hard as I could, finally yanking it open. Unfortunately, there was a metal hook attached to the door at the exact height of my forehead. The impact was so great that I literally saw stars. I staggered over to the sink and looked at my face in the mirror. I had an enormous, egg-sized lump smack in the middle of my forehead. It was changing colors and growing larger by the minute.

I staggered out and went to rejoin Neil, who looked at me with alarm, assuming I had been assaulted. I explained the situation and we asked the owner for some ice wrapped in a cloth napkin to prevent any further swelling. We left and headed back to the hotel, me pressing the ice to my wound, Neil muttering aloud, "I can't even let you go to the ladies' room by yourself."

It was weeks before the swelling went down and the many-colored bruise disappeared. Luckily, I wore my hair with bangs on my forehead. But the memory remains sharp and when I am faced with a similar situation, I open the stall door with the greatest of care. Who says you can't learn from experience?

Curses!

There is an old expression, "swears like a fishmonger." I can attest to its truth, having been married to a fishmonger for almost half a century. Neil has been working from home for the past twenty-five years using a speakerphone, so believe me when I say I've heard it all. About twelve years ago, my mom was visiting, reading the newspaper in the living room while Neil conducted business over the phone with his cousin in the adjacent dining room. She had raised us in a home where swearing was totally forbidden and was clearly horrified at the language she overheard. I quietly suggested to Neil that they tone down the conversation out of respect for my mom. At which point his cousin Michael began carefully spelling out each and every curse word. "Does he really think I can't spell?" she asked Neil incredulously after he hung up. Through the intervening years, she loved to tell that story.

Nowadays, everyone seems to swear like a fishmonger. It's hard to find a movie that doesn't have "bad" language, not to mention a cable television program. It's part of the general coarsening of our culture. Cursing doesn't bother me particularly, though I think it shows a lack of imagination or laziness on the part of the speaker or writer. I think of casual cursing in a film to be like punctuation marks, as my friend Gary puts it. After a while, you barely notice it.

The U. S. Supreme Court, also known as SCOTUS, recently heard a case about swearing on broadcast television. Everyone bent over backwards to avoid actually saying the word involved aloud. (Hint: It's a four letter Anglo-Saxon word for sexual intercourse that has been around since at least the 1600s) This is not the first time SCOTUS has discussed the issue. In 1971, it heard a case involving a man who was arrested for wearing a jacket into a courtroom in Los Angeles with a catchy three-word phrase deemed "offensive." In the general presentation for the defense, the argument was made that "the defendant was not actually suggesting having sexual intercourse with the Selective Service." A divided court acquitted the defendant but avoided using the key word in its opinion. One of the most liberal justices voted against acquittal with the reasoning that he couldn't possibly imagine his wife hearing "that word."

How the culture has changed since then. Words that were once considered "obscene" are ubiquitous now, in songs, television, movies, and everyday life. Through their overuse, they have completely lost their ability to shock. What I find shocking nowadays is the wide-spread sexual abuse of children by monsters disguised as human beings, like Jerry Sandusky, numerous Catholic priests and other adults. Those acts and their cover-ups are the true obscenities of our time. They deserve our outrage, not some overused curse words.

Condo Living

There are many advantages to living in a condo, but it is definitely not for everyone. If you are sensitive to noise, it is not for you. If you're a gardener, your terrace will not suffice. If you don't believe in following rules, do everyone a favor and buy a house. On a large plot of land.

But if you are a social creature, a condo is a good choice. If you want beautiful views but no responsibility for landscape work, condos are for you. If you pay your maintenance fees on time, you'll be welcome at any condo I know of.

The key to a well-run condo is an excellent manager and staff. The Board of Directors is almost irrelevant in a well-run condo association. Their job is to oversee things and then let the manager do his or her job with minimal interference. Unfortunately, there are many bad managers around, so weeding them out is essential. We've had probably a dozen different managers since our condo opened in 1988, running the gamut from excellent down to incredibly bad. One kept 911 on speed dial and would call at the drop of a hat. Not a good way to run a building! Another double-dipped on a regular basis, taking money from petty cash for things that had already been paid for with an association check. This is less uncommon than you would think.

If you decide to buy a condo, make sure you examine recent financial statements. Look at the reserve funds available for major replacements. See if there is working capital on hand. Check the most recent audit to see how it matches up against that year's budget. All of these documents are available for potential buyers. This information will make you an informed buyer.

Once you live in a building, if you are dissatisfied with the way the association is being run, do something. Anybody can sit back and complain (and they do). Run for the board. Talk to your neighbors. Start a letter writing campaign or get other residents' e-mail addresses, a faster and less expensive way to keep everyone informed. (This is one of the advantages of modern technology.) Become a part of the solution, instead of the problem. Be prepared for opposition from those in power. It can be brutal and you need to grow a thick skin. But it can be done. I know because I've done it. Twice.

After a period of service on the board, step back and let others lead, even if you don't have term limits. No one is irreplaceable and new blood is always welcome. (As long as it isn't splattered on the walls!)

The key to condo living is that all residents should feel welcome. If you can accomplish that, then all your effort will have been worth it.

Clothes Horse

When you are the second girl in a family of four followed by two younger brothers, you don't get to buy a lot of new clothes. You have to settle for a lot of "hand-me-downs." (To this day I have an aversion to consignment shops and even "vintage" clothing.) As a result of the new clothing deprivation during my childhood, I can't remember a time when I wasn't fashion obsessed. In high school, I envied the "in" crowd girls their perfectly coordinated sweater sets and plaid skirts, their matching knee socks and Weejuns. I went shopping to the Paramus Mall with a friend once, and remember feeling awestruck when Barbara's dad instructed her mom that they could spend up to $100, a fortune in 1959. I babysat a lot during my teens and worked at Bamberger's department store in the summer, always with the goal of improving my wardrobe while, of course, using my employee discount.

When I arrived at college, one look into my roommate Anna's closet told me I had a long way to go. It was filled with beautiful clothes, rich fabrics, intricate patterns and bright colors. My clothes looked dowdy and drab by comparison, and I've spent the last four decades trying to catch up. My husband doesn't give a hoot about his clothes, as long as they are comfortable, so he can't empathize with my clothes obsession. But he has learned to live with it and has stopped asking questions when the bills come due.

I didn't really settle on a style until the mid-1970s, when a glance at the heap of clothing on the counter of the local dry cleaners showed that virtually all of my clothes were either beige or khaki. Yikes! I needed color. Patterns. Pizzazz! I set about remedying the situation and have been working hard at it ever since. During my years as a journalist, I got into the habit of buying clothes through catalogues and have continued to do so. It's a way of dressing differently from your neighbors, because instead of shopping at the local mall, you literally have the world at large to choose from. I have catalogue purchases that are twenty years old and still look great on me. In my opinion.

My style is evolving as I age. I'm getting a little bit more like Neil in that comfort is becoming a factor. But I still am drawn to beautiful colors, rich fabrics and exotic prints. What's "in style" is much less important than what looks good on me and makes me feel good about myself. And an outfit is rarely finished until I add the crowning touch. The perfect accessory, usually a pretty necklace or colorful scarf. Then I feel ready to go out the door and face the world. Putting my best foot forward.

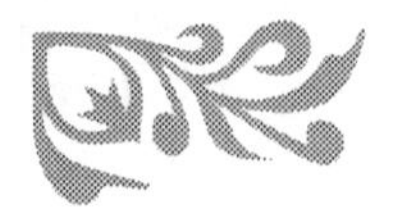 

Cayamo!

Theme cruises are a growing trend. My husband is hugely averse to the idea of spending seven days "trapped" on a boat, but when he learned about the Cayamo cruise last year, he signed us up. The main attraction would be live performances by some of our favorite singer/songwriters. John Prine was at the top of our list along with Iris DeMent and James McMurtry. In all, there were thirty musicians or groups aboard the Norwegian Pearl, including Lyle Lovett, John Hiatt, Lucinda Williams and the Civil Wars. The Civil Wars had to leave the cruise early to attend the Grammy Awards where they performed and accepted two trophies.

Two thousand music fans from all over the country gathered in Miami for this annual event. Most of the passengers were middle-aged baby boomers. Many of the men sported long hair and more than a few of the women were colorfully tattooed. There was a "hippie night" on Thursday, but, in truth, every night was "hippie night" as tie-dyed shirts and sandals predominated.

There was music all day and well into the night, in venues both large and small. There were guitar workshops and amateur contests. The cruise was billed as "A Journey Through Song" and the stops in St. Maarten, Cayo Levantado and St. Bart's seemed superfluous. The blackjack tables were empty, the dealers standing around like grooms deserted at the altar. This cruise was all about the music. My personal highlight was a John Prine concert that we viewed from front row center. Near the end of his set, Iris DeMent joined him for "In Spite of Ourselves," "Paradise" and "Unwed Fathers." It was sheer bliss. We laughed, we cried, we felt, which is what great music accomplishes when properly performed.

Cayamo, now in its fifth year, caters to blue grass/country music lovers with a little rock and roll thrown in, but there are cruises that appeal to all different kinds of musical tastes, including jazz and opera. If that's your thing, I suggest you book yourself onto the next available cruise. I promise you won't be bored. Just bring along plenty of loose fitting clothes, tie-dyed or otherwise, because the other main event between performances is eating with a capital "E." Go. Enjoy. Follow your bliss.

Cancer the Crab

I hate my sign. Really. Because I was born on June 25th, I am a Cancer. I am also a crab. I can't think of anything good about cancer. It's a disease. I've had it. Neil's had it. My mom and my aunt and my father-in-law died of it. So did a lot of my good friends. I hate cancer.

Then there's the crab. When you call a person a crab, it is not a compliment. It means they are cranky, and who wants to be around cranky people? Not me. As far as the actual crab, we used to go crabbing at Rehoboth Beach in Delaware when we were kids. I don't remember catching many crabs, or ever eating one, but I do remember falling off the pier once and being scared to death that the crabs would bite me. Luckily, they didn't.

The crab itself is not a pretty sight. It's like a spider with all those legs. Or a giant tick. It walks sideways which seems like a sneaky thing to do. Much to my surprise, I have developed a taste for soft-shelled crabs in recent years when they are fresh and properly cooked. Which is almost never. There's another kind of crab, the ones that can be transmitted between sex partners. Not a good thing to get.

To sum it up, I hate both parts of my sign. Had I been born five days earlier, I could have been a Gemini. Now that's a sign. Gemini. So distinguished that they named a rocket program after it. And the twins. Who wouldn't want to be twins? An air of mystery. A relative rarity. Much, much better than a crab. If only I had been born on June 20th.

Luckily, I don't believe in astrology. And yet I find myself looking at my horoscope more days than not. Under Cancer the Crab. That's me.

The Fabulous Bette

There are lots of amazing performers, but a few go beyond greatness. The adoration of the masses can cause many performers to self-destruct at an early age. Fortunately, Bette Midler isn't one of them. She is a survivor and has been consistently entertaining her many fans over a career that spans more than forty years. She can sing. She can act. She can tell a bawdy joke like nobody's business. She is bigger than life, a powerhouse packed inside a tiny body.

I first saw her perform on an obscure television show hosted by Burt Bacharach in 1973. She sat by a window singing her heart out in her unique interpretation of Karen Carpenter's "Superstar." She took this rather ordinary song and made it her own. It was riveting. I couldn't wait to see her perform in person.

As her star rose, she took Broadway by storm, performing in a hit show, *Clams on the Half Shell Revue*. Once was not enough for me. I dragged Neil back for the final performance. The audience just couldn't get enough of her. She made their spirits soar with "You Gotta Have Friends." She touched their hearts with "Hello in There" and the haunting "Shiver Me Timbers." Her Sophie Tucker jokes made the crowd gasp then roar with laughter. The standing ovation seemed to go on forever.

Then came *The Rose*, a movie loosely based on Janis Joplin's rise and fall. Bette was nothing short of magnificent in the role, and her versions of "When a Man Loves a Woman" and "The Rose" became instant classics. She later went on to conquer Las Vegas and tour around the country and the world. We caught her act in Miami where she just killed. "Hello Jews and queens, my people," she greeted the sell-out crowd and we ate it up. She was Johnny Carson's last guest on the venerable *Tonight Show* and she actually brought tears to his eyes, no easy task, with her rendition of "One for My Baby."

Instead of losing herself in the process like so many other big stars, Bette has achieved a remarkable balance in her life. She married and raised a daughter, who looks like a mini-me version of Bette. She quietly threw herself into projects to beautify and clean up New York and its parks. Without fanfare, she has really made a difference in her community and the world at large. Bette Midler is a perfect example of a life well lived.

Heaven Bound

I am going to heaven. Really. It doesn't matter what I do or what I believe in. I have a certificate signed by Pope Pius X guaranteeing passage to heaven for all the descendants of my maternal grandmother, Marcella Zeimis. Her brother, my mom's uncle, was a Catholic priest, who worked at the Vatican back in the 1940s and 1950s. Hence the document signed and sealed guaranteeing passage to heaven for me, and my three siblings. "But not you, Neil," my mother teased at a family reunion when she gave the rest of us copies of the elaborate certificate for posterity.

If this doesn't prove the absurdity of organized religion, I don't know what does. Just think about it. If you have the right connections, you'll get into heaven no questions asked. If you kill and torture and commit dastardly, unspeakable acts, then become "born again," or confess and show repentance on your deathbed, you'll go to heaven. But if you live an honest life, caring for others, contributing to the common good, but don't "accept Christ as your personal savior" because you are Jewish or Muslim or, God forbid, an atheist, you're going straight to hell. Really? This is what the majority of Americans believe? Really?

Religion is a very touchy subject for most people. After all, it is based on faith, not reason or proof, which is why so many scientists are non-believers. As are many, but not all, intellectuals. Two things keep religion going in the 21st century. The fear of death and the desire to be reunited with departed loved ones. I can understand these very human emotions. Sometimes I even envy true believers just a little bit. But when you step back from organized religion and examine it rationally, it just looks like a giant con game, or Ponzi scheme, where promises are made in exchange for cash. Tithe now and live forever!

Thanks, but no thanks. If there *is* an eternity, I'm spending it with Neil.

Death With Dignity

I'm unafraid of death. After all, we all die someday. It is inevitable. Part of being a conscious human being is the knowledge that you will die eventually.

What I am afraid of is Alzheimer's. My dad died of this terrible disease and watching his slow slide into oblivion was unbearable. During the period between his diagnosis in 1993 and his death five years later, it took all the courage I could muster just to visit him, especially as his awareness declined. My father was gone in every sense of the word long before his body officially died. The spark, the essence of his personhood, what someone religious might call his soul, had flickered and died out. That is what Alzheimer's does; it robs you of everything that makes you who you are long before death. Some call it the long goodbye. I think that is too kind a term for such a terrible process.

I feel strongly about end of life issues and have for many years. Jack Kevorkian was a hero of mine. People came to him for help and he provided it, even though it was technically against the law. One of the first patients he helped was a woman named Janet who had been recently diagnosed with Alzheimer's. She had watched her parents die of the disease and wished to end her life early rather than put her family and herself through the ordeal she knew would come. It was a brave, informed choice on her part, one that I hope I'm capable of making if I ever face similar circumstances.

Jack Kevorkian is no longer with us but hopefully other doctors will make themselves available to fill his shoes and help people who are terminally ill die with dignity. Because in the end, there is no less dignified a death than that of an Alzheimer's victim.

Mom and Dad in Cape Cod in 1992, celebrating their 50th anniversary

The Disappearing Thank You Note

The first writing I ever did was to take pen or pencil in hand to print thank you notes for gifts I had received. My mother was adamant about our doing this task and there were rules. You had to mention the gift, extol its virtues, and add a personal note about the person or persons who sent it.

One of my earliest notes somehow made it into my "memory box." It was laboriously printed on lined paper. "Dear Aunt Doris May and Uncle Henry, Thank you for the doll you sent for Christmas. I named her Sally. I hope you had a nice holiday. Love, Paula." My mother would look over these notes before stamps were affixed and they were sent off, promptly of course. It was always necessary to mail the thank you notes within days of receiving the present. Chores and playtime could wait. The writing of these notes came first.

It was a valuable lesson for us, one that I have followed all my life. If people take the time to choose a gift, the least the recipient should do is respond so that the giver knows the gift was received and appreciated. It is a simple equation with the receiver still ahead at the end of the process. Plus it demonstrates proper etiquette and good breeding.

Alas, the times have changed and not for the better. The hand-written thank you note is almost as rare now as a black-and-white TV. After a wedding, you are lucky if you receive a mass mailing with a generic "Thank you for your wedding gift." Period. So when I do receive a personal, hand-written note, which happens on rare occasions, I appreciate it all the more. And its sender always goes up in my estimation. I know there was a parent in the background of this person's life, teaching them the rules of proper etiquette and common decency.

Politics and The Press

Politics is in my blood. It just is. I wasn't born into a political family. It was something I stumbled into as a teenager and it quickly became my passion. Even the quote under my picture in my high school yearbook was a reference to politics, and more than a few classmates predicted I would become the first female President. That obviously didn't happen for a whole lot of reasons, but I have always been and always will be a political animal.

My chosen profession was journalism, which is something I am also passionate about. I can't start my day without the New York Times. *I just can't. Fortunately, it is now available in virtually every part of the country so I can get my hands on it every day when we travel. It's available on line too, but that doesn't count with me. I need the real thing, even though the ink stains my fingers. My idea of a perfect morning is surrounding myself with newspapers. The first stories I turn to are always political in nature. Then I turn to the Op-Ed page. It was Anna Quindlen who first introduced me to the fact that women could write brilliant opinion pieces that incorporated their personal experiences as females into the work. She eventually left the* Times *for other writing opportunities, but now Maureen Dowd and Gail Collins ably fill her shoes, writing in their unique voices twice weekly. Reading their essays is such pleasure, akin to having a conversation about politics with your smartest, most well-informed friend.*

Memories of Camelot

I remember the day I fell in love with politics. It was the summer of 1960 and the Democratic Convention played endlessly on our family's black-and-white TV. My sister picked her favorite candidate and I picked mine, Senator John F. Kennedy. When I watched him clinch the nomination and address the crowd, I was hooked. It was politics for me. Fifty years later, I am still hooked, although a little less naive.

People thought I chose Kennedy for his looks, but it was always about his mind. When he spoke, he stirred something within me and I wasn't the only one. I saw him in person only once, near the end of the campaign in November of 1960. The armory was packed to the rafters and the candidate was hours behind schedule. When he finally arrived, a roar went up from the crowd, like nothing I had ever heard before or since. It was goose bump time. His voice was hoarse from the long campaign but the words he spoke were irrelevant. Just sharing time and space with this man was reward enough for our long wait.

After the inauguration, I remember rushing home from school to watch his many press conferences. Let others tune in to *American Bandstand.* I was watching an early version of *An American President.* He was funny and thoughtful and wise. He made me proud to be an American. He was obviously enjoying himself as he bantered with members of the press corps, generally coming out on top.

Many years later, I watched videotapes of those same press conferences at the JFK Library in Boston. In hindsight, he was just as witty and smart and informed as I remembered.

That mutual respect between the press and our elected officials is sorely lacking in today's world and we are all the poorer for it.

November 22, 1963

The younger generation measures itself by 9/11. That was the before and after event that changed their lives forever. For our parents, it was Pearl Harbor Day. For my generation, it was November 22, 1963.

I was a senior at Glen Rock High School in New Jersey. I had applied for early admission into American University and was anxiously waiting to hear from them. I was eager to get to Washington and become a part, however small, of John Fitzgerald Kennedy's New Frontier.

A Spanish party was scheduled for that afternoon. My best friend Kathy and I had spent many hours the night before putting the finishing touches on a *pinata* we had created that was almost an exact replica of our Spanish teacher's head. I could not wait for the final bell to ring so we could unveil our masterpiece for all to admire. By two o'clock, there was a buzz in the hallways and rumors began to fly. Something about President Kennedy, and Dallas, and gunshots. Time stood still. We crowded around one of the few televisions in the school until our worst fears were confirmed. President Kennedy was dead. It was official. I later learned that in some schools around the country, students cheered when they heard the news. Luckily, mine wasn't one of them.

Unbelievably, classes were not called off and there was no official announcement. I went to gym class where I played the role of responsible adult, reassuring tearful classmates that everything would be okay. The country would move forward with Lyndon Johnson as our new president. The words felt hollow and unreal as I heard myself saying them.

The Spanish party was cancelled and Kathy and I allowed Mr. Vedova to take the *pinata* home to his wife intact. I arrived at my house to find my acceptance letter from AU in the day's mail. The irony did not escape me.

Life went on but it was never the same. I retained my love of politics but I decided to become an observer of the political process rather a participant. It seemed like the safer path to follow in this new post-assassination world.

My Byline

Every writer remembers his or her first byline. Mine was on the front page of the *Glen Cove Record-Pilot.* Naturally, there was a big snowstorm the day the paper first appeared on the newsstands, but nothing could keep me from driving the treacherous roads up to Locust Valley to buy a copy or two for posterity.

It wasn't long before I was offered a job as editor of another local weekly, the *Oyster Bay Enterprise-Pilot.* Now my name was on the masthead on the editorial page along with my photo, taken by the outgoing editor, Susan Francy-Jenkins. The job came with my own tiny office on South Street in the heart of the hamlet of Oyster Bay. During my tenure there, I came to love everything about this sleepy little town. Its history linking it to President Theodore Roosevelt, who summered there every year at Sagamore Hill and was buried nearby. The patriotic Fourth of July parades and crowded annual Oyster Festivals. The fact that unlike much of Long Island, this was a place where people stayed for decades and three generations of a family often lived within blocks of one another. And, of course, the breath-taking view of Oyster Bay Harbor that greeted me every day on my way to work.

I stayed at this job for more than two years until I wrote an article about the local school board, which had come under heavy criticism by the New York State Department of Education for its ties to the Republican Party among other things. I wasn't fired outright, but most of my autonomy was taken away by the head of the conservative chain of newspapers I worked for. And so, I left that post, and, several months later, started up my own weekly, the *Oyster Bay Observer.*

Now I was a writer, an editor and a publisher, wearing many hats. It was not just a full-time job. There was very little time in my life for anything else. "This is a good job for a single woman," my husband said helpfully. He was keeping the home fires burning and tending the kids, having left Fulton Fish Market a few years earlier, burned out after years of waking up in the pre-dawn hours. I was feeling torn and guilty and completely exhausted and overwhelmed. And then my former boss helped put me out of my misery by mailing his weekly paper free to all local residents. Game over! Goliath had slain David, burying her under a mountain of free newspapers. It was a valuable lesson. Be careful what you wish for. My dream of owning my own newspaper had turned out to be a nightmare.

And so I went back to writing, my first love. "I see your byline all over the place!" exclaimed a neighbor. It was true. I was free-lancing for a Long Island magazine, interviewing local notables. One of them was Sandy Chapin, Harry Chapin's widow. I interviewed her in her Huntington Harbor home. A cookie jar in the shape of a taxi caught my eye, a gift from a friend who greatly admired his signature song, a personal favorite of mine.

I was also writing more personal pieces, which were published in the *New York Times* and *Newsday*. It was a very gratifying period in my life and much less stressful than editing and publishing. I could make my own hours and had to answer to no one. And every time I picked up a publication and saw my byline, I got a thrill. Not quite the same as the first one in 1984, when I was new to the publishing game. But a thrill just the same.

New editor named

Paula Smith has been named as the new editor of the Oyster Bay Enterprise-Pilot by Karl V. Anton Jr., publisher of Long Island Community Newspapers.

Mrs. Smith replaces Susan Francy-Jenkins, who is leaving to pursue a career in public relations and photography. Ms. Francy-Jenkins was the first editor of the paper when it began being published eight years ago after a lapse of many years. The Enterprise-Pilot was Oyster Bay's first newspaper, first published in 1885.

Mrs. Smith has been employed at several local newspapers as a writer and associate editor, including the Glen Cove Record-Pilot. She is a graduate of Queens College, where she earned a bachelor's degree in political science with a minor in journalism.

A resident of the area since 1977, Mrs. Smith has been active in many local organizations including the Brookville Parent Council, Parent-School Partnership, and Locust Valley Committee on the Handicapped. She also volunteered in many capacities for United Cerebral Pals over the past 12 years.

Mrs. Smith and her husban live in Upper Brookville wit their two sons, Michael an Willis.

Paula Smith

Inaugural Bliss and Blues

I never attended a high school prom. Frankly, I'd never given it much thought, and since I rarely dated in high school, it's not so surprising that I was never asked to a prom. High school proms just weren't on my radar screen. I didn't realize this was something I had in common with Gilda Radner until Neil and I saw her show on Broadway in 1979, which ended with the stage redecorated as a giant gymnasium with streamers and balloons and a banner declaring "Class of 1964." Gilda beamed through her tears as she finally realized her lifelong dream.

Me, I was holding out for attending an Inaugural Ball. I was able to realize my dream in 1993, thanks to a series of coincidences and connections. I worked hard as a volunteer for Bill Clinton and was an active member of Emily's List, an organization aimed at electing pro-choice female candidates to public office. I casually mentioned to my mom that I had received an invitation from Emily's List to attend a luncheon in Washington during inauguration week. She strongly urged me to go. Then I mentioned to my neighbor and dear friend Jody that I was going to the inauguration. "Let me see what Ed can do," she said. I knew that Ed was the head of ASCAP, a lobbying organization for the music industry, but I had no idea he could make miracles happen. Before I knew it, I had an invitation to a private luncheon meeting on Capitol Hill with Senate Majority Leader George Mitchell, plus a box seat at the New England Inaugural Ball!

I left Florida beside myself with excitement. Neil couldn't accompany me due to a recurring back injury so I flew to D.C. solo. I was so afraid of the airline losing my luggage that I crammed everything into one carry-on bag, even my carefully chosen inaugural gown. I met with my congressman (whom I had voted against) as scheduled, to collect my official invitation to the inaugural ceremonies. The Emily's List luncheon at the Washington Hilton, where I also stayed, was very exciting, and my tablemates included the brilliant author Molly Ivins and "Dr. Ruth" Westheimer.

Inauguration Day dawned bright and sunny and I joined the masses at the outdoor swearing-in ceremony. It was a peaceful, happy crowd from all over the country. A feeling of camaraderie filled the crisp January air. Then it was back to the Hilton to take a long, hot bath and prepare for the Inaugural Ball. I was beginning to feel like Cinderella. And then, just as I finished my primping, disaster struck. I was chewing a piece of gum to calm my nerves when the cap on one of my two top front teeth came off. It was a crown that had lasted for at least ten years, one that had never given me a moment of trouble. I smiled into the bathroom mirror. It was not a pretty sight. I looked less like Cinderella and more like one of her ugly stepsisters. I summoned my inner "confident ballerina" and pushed the cap back on, holding my breath, praying it would stay on throughout the evening.

The New England Ball was a blast. The only dancing I observed was done by the new President and First Lady, followed by the new Vice President and his wife, Tipper. I sipped champagne with my box mates and we exchanged life stories. After a while, I forgot about my wayward tooth but carefully avoided eating any food just in case. On the flight home the following morning, the cap came off again and this time would not stay on. I wrapped it carefully in a tissue and kept my mouth shut until the plane landed in Fort Lauderdale. I sought out a local dentist as soon as possible, finding one who promised "gentle dentistry." I amused her office staff by recounting my inaugural adventure in detail and the case of the loose tooth.

Almost twenty years later, Dr. Silvia Stambler still kids me about the occasion that first brought me to her. The new crown still holds, as does the memory of my dream come true, my first Inaugural Ball.

Purposeful Confusion

The presidential election year 2000 was a difficult one for Florida Democrats. We had been living in Florida during the winter months since 1988 and had been voting there since 1990. Every election went smoothly until that one. I've been trying to put into words what went wrong, not only in my own Aventura precinct but in other parts of the state, and then in a recent *Newsday* article, I came across the phrase that perfectly sums up the situation: purposeful confusion. The reference concerned a Bayville, N.Y. village election, but describes exactly what happened in Democratic precincts like mine in 2000.

Keep in mind that the governor at the time was Jeb Bush, brother of the Republican candidate for president, and he had promised to deliver the state to George W. Bush. And as the late Tim Russert said over and over, blackboard in hand, the election would hinge on the results in one state: Florida, Florida, Florida. As a student of government, I take voting very seriously and have never failed to vote in any election. Every election prior to 2000 and since has gone smoothly, but in 2000, chaos reigned. We live in a Democratic precinct, and instead of the usual orderly process, there was total confusion. I went to vote early and the line was very long and moved at a snail's pace. Instead of the usual familiar faces, strangers sat at the long tables and took an inordinate amount of time to find our names in the voting roster. Several long-time voters were told they weren't registered and, if they protested loudly enough, were given provisional ballots. It was only later that we learned that the state had hired a Texas company without fanfare to purge the rolls of felons and everyone with a similar name to a felon. Hundreds of thousands of names were removed from the voting registers, almost all of them Democrats.

Unsurprisingly, voting went smoothly in Republican areas of the state. Unlike many other states, Florida is a true purple state, divided into areas that are strongly Democratic and strongly Republican, so it was an easy task for someone to organize purposeful confusion in those precincts most likely to vote for Gore. And they did. Masterfully.

Many people had gotten off the line in Aventura that morning in order to get to work. I was among the ones who stayed for the hour-long process, then went back later with Neil and Mike, and again the movement of the line was glacial. We would learn later about the infamous hanging "chads," about the butterfly ballot in Palm Beach County which caused thousands of voters to mark their ballots for Pat Buchanan, which even he admitted was not their intention. About the flyers handed out in black neighborhoods with the wrong voting day. About the thousands of ballots in Democratic areas which showed voting for every office except the presidency. This is called "under-voting" and takes place when chads from previous elections clog things up so the top of the ballot (the presidency) doesn't register a vote.

The state was originally called for Gore based on exit surveys. When the results didn't confirm those polls, the blame was placed on the company that conducted the exit polls and it was fired. We all lived in a state of limbo for the month following the election. Ultimately, the Supreme Court stepped in to stop the recount and declare George W. Bush the forty-third president. And the following month, the man who had lost the popular vote by more than half a million votes took the oath of office as Jeb Bush stood by, smiling broadly. He had made good on his promise to his brother. "Purposeful confusion" had won the day.

Unsigned Letters

What is it about an unsigned letter that leaves the recipient feeling soiled? I never received an unsigned letter until I moved into our Florida condominium. The first few years were uneventful, even peaceful. But then the atmosphere changed. Opposition to the board and manager arose. People who spoke up at meetings began receiving "Asshole of the Month" certificates in the mail. Unsigned, of course. One of the recipients was a close friend, an elderly widow who eagerly opened the letter, which was cruelly marked on the envelope "Happy Mother's Day from Your Children." She called me, shaking with fear. I felt nothing but rage towards the coward who would prey on elderly neighbors, usually women, in such a mean way.

Never one to back away from a good cause, I threw myself into the fight against the "powers that be." I started a newsletter with my name on the masthead. My husband and I conducted a town hall meeting. We instigated a revolution. The fight was on.

A few days before the election of the 1994 board of directors, I went down to the lobby for the mail and there it was, an unsigned letter with no return address. About me. About my husband. About our children. Vile accusations and insinuations. Unspeakable allegations and ugly lies. Unsigned, of course, and mailed to every resident of the building using mailing labels procured from the management office. I felt sick to my stomach. The phone started ringing. People showed up at my door, expressing sympathy as if someone had died. In truth, a part of me did die that day. Paradise had a dark side after all.

We went on to win the election. Our "slate" was elected in a landslide. I received the second highest vote total of the fifteen candidates. The board president came in last. The good guys won. We hosted a spontaneous and boisterous victory party in our apartment.

I served on the board for four years, leaving just before the birth of our grandson in 1998. I decided to run for the board again in 2006, when difficult financial circumstances and discontent with the management called for major changes. Shortly before that election, another unsigned letter appeared on my door, accusing me of being the problem not the solution. Unsigned flyers also appeared on the tables on the elevator landings warning of "chaos" if I was elected. Friends helped me remove the flyers before most of the residents could see them, but I have to admit, my feelings were hurt.

Despite the determined but anonymous opposition, I was elected to the board and accepted the role of board president. The four years that followed were peaceful for the most part. The predicted "chaos" never came about. And then on the morning of the annual budget meeting in November of 2011, I found another unsigned letter on my door. It was typed, but the grammar and spelling were so atrocious that it was hard to ascertain the author's point. I brought it to the manager and we decided to just ignore it.

That evening's meeting went pretty smoothly. There was some griping about the proposed maintenance fee increase and the fact that the new budget included modest salary increases for most of the employees. During the final "Good and Welfare" portion of the meeting, a resident approached me with a copy of the unsigned letter. He held it out to me and asked for my response. Then I did something that surprised even me. After declaring that unsigned letters are not worth the paper they are printed on, I tore it in half and returned it to him. Audible gasps from the audience. The gavel in my hand came down with a satisfyingly loud thud. Meeting adjourned!

Illegal Smile

Our jails and prisons are filled with people, mostly minorities, whose only crime is possession of marijuana. Marijuana, also known as cannabis, is a plant that has been around for centuries. It is a naturally grown substance and was not made illegal in this country until the Marijuana Tax Act of 1937. Prior to that time, it was used medicinally in many countries for various purposes, reportedly including the alleviation of the menstrual cramps of Britain's Queen Victoria. Despite the 1937 law, which effectively banned marijuana use in the U.S., musicians and other artists continued to use it in the 1940s and 1950s to enhance their creative processes.

In the 1960s and 1970s, it became the drug of choice for many baby boomers, replacing alcohol, which was favored by our parents' generation. The main difference between the two is that while countless people have died through the years from alcoholism, not one person has ever died from marijuana use. Not one. And yet it remains illegal despite the recommendations of various commissions and spokesmen as disparate as Pat Robertson, George Schultz and Bill Maher. Plus, a majority of Americans now favor either legalization or decriminalization of marijuana in poll after poll.

Singer/songwriter John Prine's tongue-in-cheek ode to marijuana, titled "Illegal Smile," describes marijuana as a means to "escape reality." You can Google the lyrics to fully understand his point of view. When he plays the song in concert, the crowd sings along with gusto. Baby boomers still partake, as do many of their adult children. In several instances, we have contemporaries who have confided to us that they hide their use from their children, and then their children confide to us that they hide their use from their parents.

As baby boomers age, marijuana continues to be the drug of choice, but now it's used not just recreationally. It is also useful for alleviating the effects of chemotherapy, HIV, migraines, chronic pain, multiple sclerosis, Parkinson's and even post-traumatic stress syndrome. Seventeen states have passed medical marijuana laws or decriminalization, in addition to Canada, Israel, the Netherlands and many other "civilized" countries. And yet our federal government outrageously continues to ignore states' rights when it comes to this issue. At a time of limited resources and prison overcrowding, this policy makes no sense whatsoever.

Where is the outrage from the conservatives who hold states' rights so dear? Where is a common sense approach when we need it the most from our politicians on the left and the right?

S.O.S.

Shortly following our move to the Salisbury section of Westbury in 1971, we learned that the local elementary school serving our neighborhood, the Salisbury School, was scheduled to be closed permanently. Concerned parents planned a demonstration to draw media attention to the situation. I made enormous signs for Mike and Will to wear, sandwich-board style, declaring "S.O.S." in huge letters and "Save Our School" below. *Newsday* sent a reporter and photographer to cover the story. The following day, there was an eye-catching photo in the paper of my two little ones wearing the signs. There was also a news article about the event, one that changed the way I viewed the press forever.

I was standing on the sidelines watching the boys when the reporter approached, asking a series of harmless questions which I answered in a straightforward way. Then at the end of the interview she asked how much I had paid for my home. "How is that relevant?" I asked, but she persisted and finally I told her the truth, which was $65,000. Now in today's market, $65,000 may not seem like much, but in 1971, it was above average, especially for houses in that particular school district. The story quoted me as saying just one thing: "I paid $65,000 for my house and we deserve to have our own school." I was horrified as I read these words, nauseated in fact. I received some angry phone calls, which I deflected as best as possible, but eventually it became yesterday's news. The school was, alas, closed despite our little demonstration. And five years later, when we moved to an area served by the Brookville School, that school was closed too only a few years after we moved there. I kept a lower profile this time. I had learned a valuable lesson about dealing with the press, one that would serve me well when I became a reporter and then an editor during the following decade.

There is a haunting scene in the film *Absence of Malice* starring the great Paul Newman and an impossibly young Sally Field, in which a woman's life is changed forever when the local newspaper reports that she had an abortion. This detail was considered necessary to a story to support a defendant's alibi. When she sees her long-held secret in print, she runs frantically through the neighborhood, collecting newspapers from front yards and porches, in a desperate and futile attempt to keep her secret from coming to light.

It is more than thirty years later, and the tragedy is that nowadays, so many in the media, print and otherwise, go for the sensational, never considering the harm they inflict on their victims. Sometimes, the truth is irrelevant. Sometimes we need to put common decency ahead of what "sells."

The Obituary

One of my earliest assignments in a journalism course was to write my own obituary. I had forgotten about it until I found it in the "memory box" my mother gave me when she and my dad moved. Uncharacteristically, I had earned only a "C" for this effort, which felt like a slap in my face. It was a bare bones account of my 18 years on planet earth. A listing of the facts: the place of birth, the names of survivors, nothing more. The punctuation and sentence structure were flawless. What was sorely lacking was any sense of the person I was or hoped to become.

It is now 46 years later and I have become a fan of the obituary. I've written my share for relatives and friends. I even composed one through tears one sleepless night eight years ago for my son Michael, as he lay comatose in a hospital bed. I collect well-written ones from the *New York Times* and *Miami Herald* about neighbors and friends, which I keep in a special black and white folder. I am always amazed at the things I find out about people I thought I knew well, especially facts about their early lives, before I made their acquaintance. After 9/11, I began each morning by reading the "Portraits of Grief" in the *New York Times* about those who had perished, my tears staining the newsprint. Each year, I look forward to the *Times'* magazine feature about the famous and less well known in the "Lives Well Lived" section.

This volume is my attempt to tell the story of my life. To make amends for that pathetic little obituary I authored as a college freshman. I've had an extraordinary life, but perhaps the same could be said for virtually everyone. After all, what would an ordinary life consist of?

My fervent hope is that in future years, this book will be appreciated by my grandson and his offspring, and they will read and reread it, and think to themselves that I was an interesting person, one worthy of remembering.

That mine was a life well lived.

Author Biography:

Paula Mack Smith is a retired journalist whose work has been published in the *New York Times*, Long Island *Newsday* and various magazines and local newspapers in Nassau County, New York. She was born in Delaware and raised in northern New Jersey. She and her husband of 45 years, Neil Smith, live in Upper Brookville, New York, and Aventura, Florida. They have two sons, Mike and Will, and a grandson, Jordan.